Encounters with God

HEAVEN
is still
FUN!

Heaven as seen by

Kim Robinson

the author of "HEAVEN is real and FUN"

For inquiries, contact:
Kim Robinson
PO Box 14
Rogers, AR 72757
www.Heavenisfun.com

Printed in the United States of America.

Edited and Designed by
Dorothea C. M. LeBlanc in 2025 (dorothealeblanc.ca)

Unless otherwise indicated, Scripture quotations are taken from the Amplified Bible Copyright © 1954, 1958, 1962, 1964, 1965, 1987 by The Lockman Foundation. Used by permission. All rights reserved.
Scripture quotations marked TPT are from The Passion Translation®. Copyright © 2017, 2018, 2020 by Passion & Fire Ministries, Inc. Used by permission. All rights reserved. ThePassionTranslation.com.
The Holy Bible, New International Version®, NIV® Copyright © 1973, 1978, 1984, 2011 by Biblica, Inc.® Used by permission. All rights reserved worldwide.
English Standard Version (ESV) the English Revised Version of 1885 (RV), the American Standard Version of 1901 (ASV), and the Revised Standard Version of 1952 and 1971 (RSV)

Pictures by UnSplashed.com

ISBN: 978-1-63618-369-5, softcover
978-1-63618-370-1, ebook

Library of Congress Control Number: 2024927652

Published by:

Avit Publishing
Lake Placid, NY 12946
518-523-1320
www.avivapubs.com

Heaven is Still FUN

"Encounters with God"

"But the one who joins himself to the Lord
is mingled into one spirit with him."
1 Corinthians 6:17 TPT

"So when that day comes, you will know that
I am living in the Father
and that you are one with me,
for I will be living in you."
John 14:20 TPT

These are personal encounters by
Kim Robinson
Author of *Heaven is real and FUN*

Heaven is still Fun

Table of Contents

Chapter 2 God Encounters

Chapter 3 Holy Spirit Encounters

Chapter 4 Animals

Chapter 5 Loved Ones

Chapter 6 Angel Encounters

Chapter 7 Other Encounters

Chapter 8 The Circus

Chapter 9 Fun with Jesus

Chapter 10 Q & A

Heaven is still Fun

Acknowledgments

I would like to thank Jerry (my husband) for his patience and grace-giving to me, which has allowed me to travel and teach. I'm also thankful for all the wonderful meals and fine dining he has provided without complaining.

Heaven is still Fun

Foreword

Endorsements from Nathan French, Yvon Attia, and Kelsey O'Malley

"What I love about Kim, is the way she makes it easy to understand the Lord's profound truths. She shares her personal, powerful encounters from a heart that says, 'This is also available to you.' Some ministers are showing their fish and saying 'Look at how big it is,' but Kim says, 'Look at how big my God is, and He's your God too.'

I take these writings of Kim's to say, 'Look at what has been made available to us through Christ, and let's explore the testimony of Jesus as the Spirit of Prophecy together. What He did for me, He can do for you. Amen.' Definitely worth the read.

Way to go Kim, you invite the 'ready to learn' to encounter God on their own."

Nathan French
nathanfrenchministries.com
awakentheplanet.com

"I have hosted Kim Robinson on Elijah Streams many times, and each time she is on the show we receive emails of testimonies of how impacted people are by her encounters. She will undoubtedly move your heart to fall into a deeper relationship with Jesus and our Father as you read her accounts of what she experienced while in Heaven. My prayer is, as you read this book your eyes would be opened to see that Jesus wants to meet with you and spend time with you. And all it takes is a YES! Enjoy reading this book as you yourself step into what Kim has seen. Read slowly and meditate on the true love of God flowing out of the pages of this book. The time for you to know him, to seek him and find him is now. "

Kelsey O'Malley
Elijah Streams Co-Host

"Kim Robinson's 'Heaven is Still Fun' is a heartfelt journey into the transformative power of encountering Jesus in the Heavenly realm. Through powerful encounters of joyfully playing in the river with Jesus, encountering God in the Throne Room, and returning to Earth with healing and restoration, Kim offers readers an inspiring invitation to experience the profound love of God for themselves. This book is more than a collection of Heavenly encounters; it's a guide for breaking through fears, receiving inner healing and discovering the truth of God's kindness. Readers will learn how to cultivate intimacy with Jesus, experience healing of the heart, and release bitterness, anger, and fear. Kim's experiences beautifully illustrate how these encounters restore identity as children of God and empower readers to walk with confidence, boldness, and love. 'Heaven is Still Fun' not only inspires but equips readers to embrace their own encounters with Heaven, unlocking freedom and renewed passion for God. With every page, Kim reminds us of the unshakable joy and peace that come from knowing God's goodness. This book is a must-read for anyone longing to experience the love of Jesus in a deeper way."

Kind Regards,
Pastor Yvon Attia
Senior Pastor of Celebrate Freedom Ministries
+1 (786) 542 4420
Yvonattia1@gmail.com
www.celebratefreedomministries.org
Facebook, YouTube, Instagram

Heaven is still Fun

Introduction

Get On Board With Encounters With God

"In the spirit realm, I kept seeing a shiny flatbed trailer with boards on the bottom, but with no sides or tailgates. I heard the Holy Spirit saying, "There's coming a new move: 'Get on board with encounters with God.' There are no sides on this trailer so you can jump on or off anytime, and there is no ceiling to box you in, or keep Him out. There is also no end to these encounters."

The Holy Spirit has been taking me to Heaven since 1988. My encounters began to happen shortly after I gave my life to Jesus and made him my Lord. In Heaven, I would meet Jesus and he would show me various fun places. We would do fun things together and he'd let me participate in many events. Afterwards, I'd write them down on paper to keep track.

On one visit I asked Daddy God, "Why are you showing me these places?" And he said, "Because people think all they do here is float around wearing diapers, eating grapes, or doing nothing but bowing before me. It's like someone is planning a party and the person you are planning it for thinks it will be boring, so they don't want to come. It saddens Me that my children don't want to come here. I have planned for each person, in detail, an eternity that will make them happy to be here with me. So you are to tell them, 'Heaven is real and fun, and Jesus is coming soon!'"

This book is about the heart of the Father; about his love for you and your love for him. You may not have known this closeness was possible with the God of Heaven — who is your Father, your Daddy, your Abba, your Papa — but he wants you to know him! So, this fun intimacy I have with Jesus is also available for you if you have asked Jesus Christ to be the Lord and Savior of your life.

The encounters that I have written are meant to encourage you, inspire you, and bring you closer to Jesus, the Father, and the Holy Spirit. Reading them can be a great way to launch you into your own encounters with Jesus, so get ready! It's time for us to unplug, turn off, slow down, and come away, to develop a relationship with the One with whom we will spend eternity.

You are not weird, strange, or crazy if you want to (or even already have) experienced encounters like those I share in this book. It's perfectly normal in God's eyes. And again, I share these encounters purely to encourage you in your relationship with Jesus, Holy Spirit, and Daddy God.

By the way, you may not find all of the events described in this book in the Bible, but you will find they do not contradict the Bible, or go against God's character, his nature, or his love for you.

This is my story; this is my journey about Heaven.

Mrs. Kim Robinson
Author of "Heaven is real and FUN"
heavenisfun.com

Chapter 1

Jesus Encounters

No More Doubt

In this encounter, I saw myself as a little girl running in a field and playing with butterflies. I felt the anointing flow down over me, removing doubt from me.

The Holy Spirit said, "Now you can receive, knowing you're not weird. Doubt causes you to not receive."

Then Jesus stood before me wanting to play, so he and I hit a beach ball back and forth.

He said, "Don't worry about your family member. I've got her in my heart." He put his hand into his heart and pulled it out.

When he opened his hand, there was a tiny person in his palm and he said again, "I've got her in my heart." Then he put his hand back inside and released her back into his heart.

My City is Blessed

During prayer, Peal (my horse in Heaven) approached me, nuzzled me and said, "We must ride." As we rode off I looked around and noticed that there was an army with us; Jesus was ahead and leading us all.

We were like a flock of geese flying in a 'V' formation, splitting darkness and shouting, "Perversion must leave! Child pornography must leave the schools – from the highest level to the lowest level! Cell phones, computers, bus drivers, janitors, and phone lines will be purified!"

Then I saw snow coming down and we all shouted, "It will be purified!" We circled a local park and I saw that gold dust had been sprinkled there.

Daddy said, "I will withhold nothing you ask for. This city is a gold mine. I'm putting you in a place that I have already designed to be a blessed city. Remember it's not you; it is ALL ME. I'm placing you here at this time and I will withhold nothing you ask for."

> Then the Lord said to Joshua, "Do not be afraid; do not be discouraged. Take the whole army with you, and go up and attack Ai. For I have delivered into your hands the king of Ai, his people, his city and his land. (Joshua 8:1 NIV)

Mirrors in My Mansion

Jesus showed me a mirror in my mansion and said, "I know how you like mirrors." It had a big frame with deep wood carvings, jewels of blue seemed to be inlaid into the wood. When we stepped in front of the mirror it didn't reflect me, there was only Jesus. But while we continued looking it began to show different things.

Jesus said, "It reflects my creation." It showed beautiful fields of flowers, waterfalls, and more.

Jesus said, "We can step into the mirror." So we did. The mirror was crystal clear and we stepped right through it, just like we do with the pictures in my mansion. Jesus and I walked around in the fields of flowers.

Grapevine

While I was soaking in Jesus' presence, instantly Jesus and I were walking on top of a beautiful mountain that overlooked an ocean. We walked to a thick, lovely and soft hanging vine. I sat on the vine wondering if it was strong enough to hold me, and then Jesus pushed me from behind on this vine-swing.

Jesus walked over and sat on some soft and bushy grass to my right. As I kept swinging on the grapevine, it would swing me out from the cliff, to right over the ocean. It was breathtaking!

Jesus said, "You wonder if the vine is strong enough to hold you."

I said, "Well, yes," as I looked far down to the ocean below.

Jesus said, "You wonder if the vine is sturdy enough."

I answered, "Well, yes," as I looked at the sharp rocks beneath me.

Jesus said, "I am strong enough to hold you up."

He reached down, took a handful of green grass and raised up his hand. He blew into the grass and it turned into tiny white birds and butterflies that flew away. His breath brought life.

Jesus said, "You don't have to worry. Just be intimate with me because I've got you. Have a close relationship with me."

Jesus reminded me of the Scriptures,

> So you must remain in life-union with me, for I remain in
> life-union with you. For as a branch severed from the vine

will not bear fruit, so your life will be fruitless unless you live your life intimately joined to mine. "I am the sprouting vine and you are my branches. As you live in union with me (your source) fruitfulness will stream from within you. But when you live separated from me, you are powerless. (John 15:4-5 TPT)

"Neither can you, Kim, bear fruit unless you remain in me," he said.

Universe

Jesus took me to a place so high I could look down and see a whole universe with all its stars and colors: pink, white, and red. It was so amazing.

With a great and very intense love for God, I kept saying, "God, this is so beautiful, this is so beautiful, this is so beautiful!" It made me want to sweep my foot across it and touch it. Daddy God was happy that I loved it, and that I thanked and praised him for his creation. His creation displays his greatness.

Lift up your eyes to the sky and see for yourself. Who do you think created the cosmos? He lit every shining star and, formed every glowing galaxy, and stationed them all where they belong. He has numbered, counted, and given each one a name. They shine because of God's incredible power and awesome might; not one fails to appear! (Isaiah 40:26 TPT)

Spirit Realm

Jesus took me to a vast open view of a beautiful land with green grass and nothing else. He said, "Nothing is growing here that you can draw from, except peace — nothing to weigh you down. There is no worry, anxiety or fear. Nothing but peace. You haven't planted anything like that here in the spirit realm. All of those live in the soul realm. If you're feeling those feelings, you live in the soul realm not the spirit realm. Live out of the spirit realm. Stay out of the soul realm and live in the spirit realm of peace."

My husband got in a car wreck later that day. I had to remember to stay out of the soul realm, stay out of worry, fear and anxiety, and just rest in the spirit realm of peace. Everything turned out and he was not seriously injured, but later he received a new car. What the devil meant for evil, God turned around for the good.

They Cheer For You

While I was worshipping, I saw the brightest white lights in the form of a cross, coming at me.

Jesus said, "It is our Father's throne." I walked towards the bright lights and stepped into that realm with Jesus. People were there, and they put a white robe on me and led me to a stage. Jesus was on the stage (you move quickly in Heaven) to greet me with a hug. He turned me around and I saw many people clapping and cheering for me.

Jesus said, "We are very proud and happy for your promotion. We are happy for you to go from Glory to Glory," and everyone cheered.

I asked, "Can you show me in the Bible where people in Heaven are happy for someone on Earth?"

I heard, "Rejoice with those who rejoice [sharing others' joy], and weep with those who weep [sharing others' grief]." (Romans 12:15 AMP)

Jesus said, "We celebrate anything and everything up here." And everyone laughed and cheered! Suddenly I stood next to a round table. The people who were sitting there began to cheer for me.

Jesus said, "They are planning your future."

I heard them laughing, shouting and clapping around the table saying, "She's going to love that!"

Ruth (from the Bible) was there, she laughed and said, "They love planning your future because you aren't the norm, and you are willing to step out and have fun."

Ball of Light

I was worshipping and soaking in Jesus's presence when I stepped into the spirit realm where Jesus met me.

He squeezed and kissed me and said, "You will have what seems to be a ball of light in your hands. I will tell you when to send it into the darkness." Then I felt like I was lifted by talons and set into a nest of the softest feathers.

Jesus said, "Rest, just rest." Then I saw myself ministering to people and they were so quickly healed.

Jesus said, "It's just that easy. You will be surprised because it's as it should be."

> He will cover you with His pinions, And under His wings,
> you will find refuge; His faithfulness is a shield and a wall.
> (Psalm 91:4 AMP)

I saw Jesus' Glory

While standing on the front porch outside of my house, my eyes were closed and I was enjoying the fresh breeze blowing by. I saw an extremely bright yet cloudy mist-like form. My eyes wanted to squint but they were already closed.

Jesus said, "This is my glory; it's as bright as the sun. The sun's brightness is symbolic of my glory."

Then I saw part of a robe with a large hand reaching out of the misty form and heard, "Come up with me." I reached out my hand and instantly I was looking down towards Earth from Heaven.

Jesus said, "There are going to be more supernatural things happening worldwide and often these things will turn people's minds towards Me. Supernatural things like arms and legs growing out, and transgender people being restored. And I'll be appearing in third world countries. There will be revivals and so much more. I will tell you before it happens. I will tell you only a day or so in advance, so you must spend time with me daily."

> While traveling on the road at noon, Your Highness, I saw the light brighter than the sun flashing from Heaven all around me and those who were with me. (Acts 26:13 TPT)

A Swing For Two

Jesus and I sat on a swing made for two. I sat in one direction and Jesus sat in the other direction. There were three ropes and we shared the middle rope. I would push off and Jesus would lift his feet, we would swing back and then Jesus would push off while I held my feet up. We swung high, as a team. Then Daddy God came to the swings and began to push us. We went even higher with the Father's power pushing us. But the three of us had to work as a team. The lesson was obvious.

> [I always pray] that the God of our Lord Jesus Christ, the Father of glory, may grant you a spirit of wisdom and of revelation [that gives you a deep and personal and intimate insight] into the true knowledge of Him [for we know the Father through the Son]. (Ephesians 1:17 AMP)

Waist High Flowers

I was worshipping Jesus and then stepped over into the spirit realm by faith. Jesus hugged me and I noticed we were standing in a field of waist high flowers. They looked like pansies, the colors were bright and vibrant. I held a flower head in my hand and noticed that the petals were pulsating and beating with life.

Jesus said, "Taste it." I pulled a petal from the deep purple flower and put it in my mouth. It tasted like Jolly Ranchers and Life Savers combined. Then I saw a yellow dandelion which was also waist high. When I tasted the dandelion it had the flavor of orange, bananas, and lemons all mixed together.

Then I tasted a bright white flower and it tasted like white! I just don't know how to describe the clean, pure white flavor it had but I could feel life and positivity coming into me. But at the same time it also highlighted the negative in my soul. I knew I needed to command all negativity out of my cells, body, lungs, organs, kidneys, heart, bladder, etc.

I began to declare life, and instantly I started to feel more joyful and alive. Even the birds outside began to sing!

> A tender, tranquil heart will make you healthy, but jealousy can make you sick. (Proverbs 14:30 TPT)

Sitting With Jesus

As I was walking up this mountain (on Earth), I found some chairs along one of the trails and decided to sit down. I couldn't believe I had finally reached Moravian Falls and Prayer Mountain, in North Carolina!

The presence of God was there; it was like what I feel when I go camping except I could tell this feeling encompassed the entire mountain.

I sat there — with Jesus sitting beside me, holding my hand. He was wearing his traditional robe and I asked him why he was wearing it.

He said, "This is how they saw Me years ago when they worshiped and prayed to me on this mountain. They would call me 'Ancient of Days.'" He was talking about the Moravian Church back in the 1700s.

Twenty Angels

While sitting quietly on a chair in the woods of Prayer Mountain, I saw what seemed like twenty angels standing before me; they were smiling and seemed to be waiting for instructions. They appeared in human form, not with enormous wings or with lightning shooting from them (like I had seen in my kitchen one time). They just stood waiting for me to say something.

I said, "Thank you God, for the angels you have given to help me." Then they instantly moved from in front of me, to behind me as if that was the assignment they had been waiting for. They were here to assist me in what God had called me to do. I could feel them standing right behind me (like I can now).

As Jesus and I walked along the top of the mountain ridge I could see a crowd of angels with large vases pouring something over me. And I could see other angels declaring blessings as I walked along the road. They continued to speak blessings and/or pour an oil substance into me as I continued walking. Sometimes the oil appeared to be liquid gold. Each time they poured and blessed I would say, "I receive. I receive from the angels of God."

The angels were clapping earlier as I had come up the road because I had finally come to receive them. They were given an assignment from God to assist me and had already been waiting a while for me to come to Prayer

Mountain to receive them. God had assigned them to me, but they had to wait for my obedience. And in order for me to receive the angels into my life, I had to obey and go where God had told me to go.

You could go to the graveyard or a bar and receive demons, or you could watch certain types of movies and receive demons. But you can also go to where God tells you to go and receive angels who are assigned to assist you. They are glad to be sent by God to minister to us to help us achieve the plans and purposes that God has created for us.

> Are not all the angels ministering spirits sent out [by God]
> to serve (accompany, protect) those who will inherit
> salvation? [Of course they are!] (Hebrews 1:14 AMP)

Jesus' Garden

Jesus took me to his garden. It had an archway of pure bright greenery and all types of flowers of all colors stretching out to him as he walked by. The foliage and flowers in Heaven have no death or brown in them. I saw the brightest, purest greens in this foliage; but they were not like the fluorescent greens created on Earth.

I put my hand in this thick, lush greenery and it wrapped around my hand. I leaned into them and laughed as they wrapped me. Jesus laughed at my discovery.

We walked over and stood looking over the most beautiful valley. This valley was covered in thick, fresh greenery (that you don't have to mow). It was so peaceful.

> And why would you worry about your clothing? Look at
> all the beautiful flowers of the field. (Matthew 6:28 TPT)

Pure Gold

This week while camping, I saw Jesus standing in the Throne Room with angels flying and filling the room (which had no walls or ceiling above). I didn't look at the angels because Jesus was before me.

His hair looked like it was maade of strands of pure liquid gold, like a gentle flowing waterfall, like shining glory, like wavy flowing gold. He stood like a King, entirely in charge, and there was nothing that could intimidate him.

His breath is pure life (not like coffee breath). It's so reassuring that he is still King and knows it. We can trust him.

> They will wage war against the Lamb, but the Lamb will conquer them, for he is Lord of lords and King of kings! Those who are with him will also conquer them, and they are called 'chosen ones' and 'faithful ones.' (Revelation 17:14 TPT)

Pinstriped Waterfall

During worship, I felt a drawing to Jesus as I stepped over into the Heavenly realm. Jesus and I stood at the bottom of a waterfall, looking up. The water was pinstriped with multiple colors of deep reds, deep purples, dark blues, rich golds, yellows, and more.

Instantly we stood at the top of the waterfall and rode the falls down into the pool below. The pinstripe water kept its lines. It didn't mix or mingle with nearby colors. Jesus and I played in the water.

Then as a big brother might do, Jesus turned over onto his stomach and said, "Get on My back. I'll give you a ride." I climbed onto his back.

I was not a child this time but more like a young adult in my 20s. As I rode on Jesus, I could feel the strength in his shoulders, arms, and back as he began to swim downstream. He swam with freestyle and butterfly strokes, while I was his passenger.

Strangely, the water still did not lose its stripes even though Jesus splashed as he swam and carried me. When the water droplets separated from the rest of the water, even each drop kept its separate color. The pinstriped water obeyed Jesus by staying in formation.

I asked Jesus afterward, "What do you want me to take back to the Earth from this experience?"

Jesus said, "I want you to take JOY back with you."

After this encounter I felt so much joy in my soul all day. I was joyful knowing Jesus always has everything under control, even in chaos.

Don't Analyze It — Enjoy It.

I saw Jesus covered in tiny birds as I stepped into Heaven. Then birds began to land all over me as I approached him. (I was remembering, with thanks, that there is no bird poop in Heaven!) Jesus smiled as he reached up with a tiny bird on his finger and gently placed the bird on my nose.

I looked at Jesus, past the bird on my nose.

He smiled and said, "Don't analyze it — just enjoy it."

Line Dancing

I had this encounter with Jesus in Heaven:

I was walking down a long hall towards a banquet or party room. I could hear laughter and happy music. As I walked into the room, I saw Jesus and others line dancing, celebrating, and laughing. They invited me to the line dance so I joined in and we all laughed and celebrated together as we danced and mingled.

It was more like a celebration and I didn't even know what we were celebrating as we danced!

> I was overjoyed when they said, Let's go up to the house of the Lord. O Jerusalem, you were built as a city of praise, where God and Man mingle together. (Psalm 122:1,3 TPT)

Rhinestone Cowboy

One time I saw Jesus in Heaven but he was not wearing the white robe that some people think he always wears. He was wearing a magnificent robe that appeared to have something like rhinestones attached to it.

After looking closer I could see they were not rhinestones but gemstones made right into the fabric. The gems had a slightly rounded surface, were the diameter of maybe an orange, and were sunken into the fabric. They were all over his robe which reached to the floor. It was a robe fit for a King! I noticed that Jesus' brown and wavy hair was shiny, as if it had just been treated with hot oil.

Some of you may remember Glen Campbell's 1975 song "Rhinestone Cowboy." It's funny but that was the first song I thought of when I saw this scene. It proves that when you are in Heaven, you still have your soul and can remember things from your past.

As I looked at Jesus, I noticed his face didn't have any brown spots, his arms didn't have liver spots, there was no darkness in or on him at all. He was pure and spotless inside and out.

I asked Jesus, "What causes us to have darkness on the inside? When I pray for people, I sometimes see darkness in or on them."

Jesus said, "Being offended causes darkness in the soul. Offenses cause bitterness in the heart."

I looked up the definition of offense: It's the act of attacking, or feeling attacked, having a poor attitude, being irritated when something is disagreeable to the eyes or unpleasant to the senses.

Offense dams up the living Water of Life in your soul and keeps it from flowing. Offense will stop the moving of the Holy Spirit. Offense can also enter our soul when the enemy has fired his fiery darts at us — and we have received them.

The enemy has brought the acceptance of bad attitudes into TV and social media and so many people just consider these attitudes as a normal feeling or response. But remember that each offense, no matter how small, brings darkness to our souls and hearts. The enemy wants us to be offended because he knows how severely it affects our hearts. If we give in to offense, then before we know it, our hearts will be full of bitterness. Bitterness is made up of hundreds of little offenses.

So pray for the spirit of offense to be broken off and removed.

Repeat this, "I repent for partnering with this demonic spirit of offense, and I break it off of me right now. I choose not to be offended. Instead, I receive love." Be quick to reject offenses and be quick to receive God's love.

> For out of his mouth speaks from the overflow of his heart. (Luke 6:45b AMP)

> Death and life are in the power of the tongue. (Proverbs 18:21 AMP)

Chapter Two

God Encounters

Sheets of Light

I saw sheets of light as if we were flying through time at a fast speed.

The Lord said, "Things are going to speed up in the spirit realm, which means they'll also speed up on Earth. I need split-second obedience. Just like when you tell your dog, 'NO, SIT!' as another car goes speeding by. A split second of disobedience makes a lot of difference. I need split-second obedience to keep this ball rolling."

Please pray this with me; "Jesus, please forgive me for disobedience, and help me to be quickly obedient each time you ask."

> While you have the Light, believe in the Light [have faith in it, hold to it, rely on it], that you may become sons of the Light and be filled with Light as followers of God. (from John 12:36 AMP)

His Goodness is as Big as the World

Sometimes I appear in Heaven as a small child, around five years old, other times I appear as an adult, but I still get to sit on Daddy's lap and feel like a child.

One time during worship I could actually feel myself sitting on Daddy's lap. He held me and we rocked. While I was there I saw a blue-like ball the size of a world.

He said, "Not many have seen it."

I asked, "Can I have it?"

Daddy said, "It's My goodness in a degree that most haven't seen. It will cause people to ridicule you and make fun of you." But I could see many getting out of wheelchairs.

I said, "I want it, if it is Your goodness. Many will believe, some will not." Then I felt it go into me.

Daddy said, "You are in a season of my favor; don't be afraid to reach out and step out. You're in MY favor."

> "And when he has come, he will convince the world of its sin, and of the availability of God's goodness, and of deliverance from judgment. (John 16:8 TLB)

Release Disappointment

I was sitting in my blue flower chair in Heaven, as Daddy God continued to whittle.

He said, "Release disappointment. You think you'll be disappointed in this too." (ie. in what he had in his hand).

I said, "Yes, but I would *act* like I like it."

He laughed and said, "Oh, you'll like what I'm making for you." He looked at me with a raised eyebrow.

Daddy God has been whittling on a stick for me for quite some time. This location (with my blue flower chair) is very peaceful and calming, and he loves to meet with me in this garden area.

When you step over into these Heaven encounters, it's a time to get free from the things you carry. The Father wants you to be with him so you can get free and then go back to Earth to carry out your assignment.

> O my God, I trust, lean on, rely on, and am confident in You. Let me not be put to shame or [my hope in You] be disappointed; let not my enemies triumph over me. (Psalm 25:2 AMPC)

Blue Skies

While taking a bath, I had a vision of God. We held hands and walked over to, and then on the blue sky. We walked through the atmosphere with the blue sky below, above, and all around us. Then we sat down on a seat that instantly appeared. He pulled me right up close and under his right arm.

Daddy said, "I was there when you were little, and I'm still here now."

I saw yellow-like flames dancing over me, going up and down.

He said, 'That's my Glory.'

Fishing with Daddy God

Daddy took my hand and we walked over and sat down to fish. He had a cane pole for himself and an extra one for me. He pulled me real close and put his arm around me.

I thought while looking at his old fashioned fishing pole, "Why don't you have a new fancy one?"

He laughed and said, "I like this."

I thought, "How do you, or I, reel it in?"

Daddy God laughed and said, "You'll have to swing it in, or pull on the string. You'll figure it out."

Then I got a bite and pulled up hard on the pole but the fish got away. You'd think that when fishing with God, I'd pull in a monster fish!

He said, "Here, you'll need some more bait."

He put a sweet square on the hook and said, 'To catch fish you must use something sweet." His eyes sparkled as he grinned. We sat there on a seat for two, fishing alone by the river. The grass was so soft and thick that I felt life below my feet. The birds sang. The sky and everything was just so beautiful. I began to cry because of the beauty and the peace.

Daddy said, "I love to fish, and that's why I called it fishing for men."

Suddenly I felt sleepy and bad for falling asleep while fishing with him.

He knew my thoughts and said, "Don't you love it when your child or grandchild falls asleep on you because they feel safe and loved enough to do that?" So I cuddled my head next to his body. I woke up later with still no fish — but I'd had a great time fishing with Daddy.

Note: A few days later my husband and I went kayaking and floated past a grey-haired fisherman. He yelled, "I just have to find what sweet bait the fish will bite."

> When you abide under the shadow of Shaddai, you are
> hidden in the strength of God Most High. (Psalm 91:1 TPT)

Daddy's Chamber

Singing in the spirit (in tongues), I felt like I was in Daddy's presence.

He said, "You have come into My Chamber. I put on you this robe. It's a robe to wear in My Chamber, a robe of purity and holiness. From this day on I give you wings, wings to soar." The robe was so thick, soft, and furry-like.

> He placed the Cherubim inside the innermost room of the temple, with their wings spread out. (1 Kings 6:27a NIV)
>
> I long to dwell in your tent forever and take refuge in the shelter of your wings. (Psalm 61:4 NIV)

A Love Story

At night during prayer, I heard Daddy God say to me, "Your life is going to be a LOVE STORY. My love is solid and powerful. My love casts out demons; it causes them to flee. My love doesn't strive. You will walk in my love and not strive. I kiss your face, including your eyes, nose, lips, cheeks, and chin. I love you with all of my heart. You will be an example of Me pouring out my love for others to witness. Your life is a love story. Yield, don't push."

> But the one who joins himself to the Lord is mingled into one spirit with him. (1 Corinthians 6:17 TPT)

Living Room in Heaven

During a worship service, I stepped over into the spirit by faith, and in Heaven I saw one large room like a living room. The furniture was incredibly soft, the design was smooth and gentle, the colors were soft and soothing, and the doorway was round and inviting — everything had a soft look to it. Walking into the next room I noticed it had a similar smooth design too.

Then Daddy God said, "I am soft and gentle."

When people come into his presence he softens their compassionless, hard hearts. People are changed each time they enter His presence. Take the time to quiet yourself and come away to spend intimate time with Jesus and the Father daily.

> But the fruit produced by the Holy Spirit within you is divine love in all its varied expressions: joy that overflows, peace that subdues, patience that endures, kindness in action, a life full of virtue, faith that prevails, gentleness of heart, and strength of spirit. Never set the law above these qualities, for they are meant to be limitless. (Galatians 5:22-23 TPT)

Waves Of Worship

One day while camping, I was studying about the Blood of Jesus and then inserted my name to make the scriptures more personal:

> And they were all singing this new song of praise to the Lamb: 'Because you were slaughtered for us (Kim), you are worthy to take the scroll and open its seals. Your blood was the price paid to redeem us (Kim). You purchased us (Kim) to bring us (Kim) to God out of every tribe, language, people group, and nation.' (Revelation 5:9 TPT)

This stirred such a boldness in me that suddenly I wanted to be with Him. And I was! I met Daddy God in his blue flower garden. He handed me so many blue flowers that I was covered with them. He was lavishing me with love.

Then just as suddenly, we were in the Throne Room. I was standing before his throne watching waves of worship like watery ribbons go around it. I saw people lay on these waves of worship and float upwards out of sight. I joined them in this effortless worship and lay down on these waves of worship.

The Father sat on his throne watching and smiling as we floated upward. These waves of worship seemed to be coming into his Throne Room but I couldn't tell if the worship was coming from Earth or Heaven itself; maybe it was a combination of both.

Cradled in His Arms

I saw the Father with an adult cradled in his arms like someone would hold an infant. The adult was in a fetal position, not scared or crying.

He said, "I cradle you in my arms. Everything I have is yours."

Daddy looked lovingly down at the "baby" in his arms like it was his first newborn and said, "Everything you will need I will provide. I now give you everything. I can't love you more because I love you so much, with everlasting love. You don't have to strive for MY love. I pour my love over you, covering you and saturating you. Receive my love. You will never have to work for my love. I give it to you freely and abundantly."

Then he said to me, "I fully love them. That is why I deliver them and provide for them. Everything happens under the covering of my love. Don't look at the storm."

Remember to stay focused (like flint) on how much the Father loves you. Fear is the opposite of love. Faith is rooted in the Father's love.

God's Blue Eyes

The Holy Spirit woke me up at 4:15 am.

I heard the Lord say, "I AM the all-seeing 'I' (not eye, but 'I'). The Illuminati is not the capital 'I', but I AM. They use the eye as a symbol and say they are the all-seeing eye. I see all, I know all, I am the 'I'. You don't have to fear the future because I will care for and provide for you. I am the capital 'I'."

Later that day I saw Daddy in the garden where we met before. I put my hands on his face and gazed into the most beautiful blue eyes. His eyes changed color. This time they looked like those blue marbles with layers of crystal blue. When you look into his eyes you can see all of eternity; they have so much depth.

Then I saw eyeballs rolling down from Heaven to the Earth! They looked like billiard balls rolling down a slide. Suddenly the Holy Spirit flashed in front of me, waving colors.

I said, "Holy Spirit, you're pretty dramatic today." He laughed as the scene changed; now colored eyeballs were rolling down from Heaven instead of black and white eyeballs.

There are those who need eyes to see, either in the natural or in the spiritual. The Holy Spirit is showing them that they are here now, from Heaven.

Put your hands over your eyes and say, "I receive my new eyes."

Brains Healed

During worship I was made aware that I was sitting in Daddy God's lap in the Throne Room. I reached out and saw that my arms were inside God's arms.

Then suddenly I saw a large, serpent-like dragon head rise up. I knew that this serpent was the cause of all brain disorders, seizures, dementia, Alzheimer's, depression, and anything that had to do with the brain.

Then I heard myself speak (but God's voice said it), "Give ME that serpent's head!" Angels from around the throne flew to the serpent, and cut off its head.

I said, "Give me his head" (but it was God's voice using my voice).

The angels brought the serpent's head to me on a platter. Then God's fire and lighting hit the serpent's head and burned it up. A wind came and blew the ashes away.

God said, "From this day on, you will hear in the news about how seizures and all brain disorders are on the decline."

Whatever the cause is: if it's from hormone imbalance, thyroid, or chemicals, the cause will be exposed and removed. The serpent is behind it all, and its head is now cut off.

Nature Reflecting The Son

While camping and looking at the water, I noticed a few sparkles reflecting the sun. God told me this is how we look to him, like sparkling diamonds reflecting his Son.

Then I saw the wind blow across the water, and the whole lake began to sparkle. I could even see a few sparkling reflections back in the dark cove. I knew he was saying these sparkles represent his people. Then the wind blew in the dark cove and there were hundreds, if not thousands of sparkles reflecting the sun/Son.

He said, "This is what I am doing now. I am blowing across the country and my children are shining for me. They are reflecting me. I am blowing into the dark coves and my children are shining. They reflect me and my love. Know that my wind is blowing and my children are shining. This isn't *going* to happen, but this is happening *now*."

Green Rolling Hills

Sitting next to Daddy God, I'm both in him and beside him; ie. half of my body is in him while the other half sits beside him. We are looking out and all I see are fresh green valleys and rolling hills covered with new green growth. There is nothing burnt, dead, or brown (no trauma, no fear), there's not even the smell or appearance of smoke in the air, only life with an atmosphere of peace and joy.

With his arm around me, Daddy said, "Those that have arrived this week? This is what they will experience: new life, peace, and joy."

> On that day [when that time comes], you will know for yourselves that I am in My Father, and you are in Me, and I am in you. (John 14:20 AMP)

Every tribe, every nation, when they step over to Heaven, will find this place of beauty.

Listen for the 'Gentle'

Daddy God is gentle.

He said, "I don't have to be harsh, demanding, or forceful because I have all power. They (speaking of the nations that are his enemies) are watching for an explosion of my power. They are not expecting my gentleness to deliver. I can stop their schemes with a gentle snowfall. I have all power. I don't need force."

"Remember, it was a gentle baby in a gentle basket in a gentle river that overtook the nation. They were watching for the army to come in violently, while the gentle was coming down the river. You don't have to be violent when you have all power and authority — ALL power. I have all power and all authority. With just the tip of my finger I can change the course of history. It wasn't a slap of my hand. It was the tip of my finger."

> Have you entered the storehouses of the snow or seen the storehouses of the hail, which I reserve for times of trouble, for days of war and battle? (Job 38:22 NIV)

Cure for Anxiety

> Therefore, I tell you, stop being worried or anxious (perpetually uneasy, distracted) about your life, as to what you will eat or what you will drink, nor about your body, as to what you will wear. Is life not more than food and the body more than clothing? Look at the birds of the air; they neither sow [seed] nor reap [the harvest] nor gather [the crops] into barns, and yet your Heavenly Father keeps feeding them. Are you not worth much more than they? And who of you, by worrying, can add one hour to [the length of] his life? (Matthew 6:25-27 AMP)

TV Room

This evening while praying, I saw Daddy God. I ran up to him and hugged his neck. A Christian man that I have never met personally in the natural, showed up. He just popped into the Throne Room and asked me if I'd like to look around.

I asked Daddy God about him and he said, "It is OK, he comes here often."

This man showed me a throne-type chair where I could sit. I did and a TV screen flashed my life before me. Then he backed out so I could watch my life, ask God for forgiveness, and purify my soul if needed. He came back in when the screen ended. We stood up and walked out.

He walked me over to the balcony edge and said, "Watch."

I was still concerned about whether I should be seeing him, but Jesus showed up and said, "It's Okay." From the balcony, I watched the atmosphere change color as worship from Earth ascended to Heaven.

Then I was taken to another taller throne-type chair where I sat to oversee local areas and family members. From this seated place, I declared: "Fire to purge souls! Fire to burn out any ungodly friends and idols! Fire to burn out the love of this world! Fire to bow its knee to God." I spoke in the spirit realm, and verbally said it out loud in the natural. It felt heavy and difficult to talk in the natural realm.

This encounter showed me that, from Heaven, I could sit in a place of authority and declare blessings and provisions over the Earth and family members. Shortly after this encounter, some family members changed drastically. They left their old ways and turned to Jesus.

Sea of Glass

I was worshiping Jesus when I felt the presence of God (or "Daddy God," as I like to call him). So by faith I leaned into that presence and stepped over into the spirit.

Note: It's all by faith: As you feel his love and presence fill the room, you can lean into it and by the Holy Spirit's leading, simply step from this realm into the spirit realm.

> And now, because we are united to Christ, we both have equal and direct access in the realm of the Holy Spirit to come before the Father! (Ephesians 2:18 TPT) The Holy Spirit is our Friend, Advocate, Standby, Counselor. He will unveil the reality of every truth. (from John 14:16 TPT, John 14:26 Message, John 15:26 AMP, John 16:13 TPT)

Instantly I was standing by Daddy God in the Throne Room. He hugged me and sat me on his lap so I could observe what he saw. From my vantage point on the Father's lap, looking out into the Throne Room I saw what appeared to be a sea of glass.

It was a vast sea that was crystal-clear, pure, and clean. I thought maybe this was the crystal sea I had read about in the Bible, but it didn't look like the watery sea I had imagined; it was something different, but a bit more like glass.

I noticed that the Throne Room was also different. People were not shouting, dancing, or celebrating; they were in total awe in the presence of God. They were overwhelmed at the goodness and love that they had now become. As I watched the saints bowing before the throne of God and worshiping, one person at a time began to sit upright from a bowed-over state.

That is when I realized the depths of what Jesus has done for us and how God actually sees us now by the blood of Jesus. Jesus has made us (the saints) pure, clean, and holy, without any darkness at all. The saints I saw had no stain, dark spots, or shame.

As they stood and came before the throne of God bowing before him, they appeared so pure, crystal clear, and transparent. I knew they were not filled with shame, they did not feel undeserving or dirty, or needing to crawl like poor saints. No, I could tell they felt pure, clean, and loved; and they wanted to love the ONE who provided it all.

The Father sat quietly filled with indescribable love in this wonderful, love-filled Throne Room. He was captured by their love and appreciation for the purity of forgiveness and wholeness that only Jesus could have provided for them.

I was then taken quietly back into the natural realm, back into my prayer room, leaving Daddy to receive the worship he so deserves.

> To him who overcomes I will grant to sit with Me on My throne, as I also overcame and sat down with My Father on His throne. (Revelation 3:21 NKJ)

> … and in front of the throne, there was something like a sea or large expanse of glass, like [the clearest] crystal. (some of Revelation 4:6 AMP)

Chapter 3

Holy Spirit Encounters

Field of Carnations

While sleeping, I had an encounter in Heaven. I ran through a field packed with carnations and pixie flowers that were about four or five feet tall. I felt free and childlike, running with Jesus without a care. I woke up feeling refreshed like I'd just returned from a relaxing vacation.

The Holy Spirit will take your spirit to Heaven or different places while sleeping because your spirit does not sleep. So if you have a busy mind or life, sometimes the night time is the best way for the Holy Spirit to speak to, and encounter you.

Holy Spirit says "Yes! Yes! Yes!"

While sleeping, I had another encounter with the Holy Spirit: He was poking my stomach with his finger as I was lying in bed.

I shook and jerked, and heard the Holy Spirit say, "YES, YES, YES."

He said, "YES, Kim, when you ask, 'Should I pray for that one?' I say, 'YES.' When you ask, 'Should I go and chase him down, the one who doesn't even see me, but I see he is hurt?' I say, 'YES.' My blessings will come and overtake you *and* them. Kim, when you ask, 'I overhear she has a pain in her hand. Should I pray for her? She's not even talking to me.' I say, 'YES, YES, YES!' When you ask, 'Should I agree in prayer and pray for them when they live so far away?' I say, 'YES, YES, YES, YES, YES, YES, YES, YES!'" It was so powerful I doubled up like I was hit in the stomach and was giving birth.

Jesus said, "I heal the undeserving, and love them without someone's approval."

He said, "YES you will be terrified if you look down so stay focused on the person you're praying for. Yes, you will be extremely terrified if you look at your surroundings. I'm not telling you that you won't. So stay focused and you won't be terrified of being on the edge of the cliff, so high up and out on the edge. Stay focused."

I said, "Thank you Jesus, thank you Jesus."

While still sleeping, God's power surged through me, over and over in my stomach. Then he said, "Look at the time." It was 1:15 and 1:17. He said, "Luke."

> ... for they will be great in the sight of the Lord...and they will be filled with the Holy Spirit. (Luke 1:15 Amp)

> And they will go on before the Lord, in the Spirit and power of Elijah... to make ready a people prepared for the Lord. (Luke 1:17 Amp)

Fire Consumes the Hurt

Tonight during prayer at home, I saw a fire coming down like a tunnel and heard, "This fire consumes the hurt. It burns out what the eyes have seen. It burns out child perversion. It burns out what their hands have done. It burns out what their mouths have said. It's cleansing the town of child perversion. This fire purifies the one that was hurt and it burns what they remember."

Then I saw chains hanging down.

People have chains of fear wrapped around themselves and their ears because they don't want to hear the silence, so they are always talking, or they're workaholics. People have chains around their hands, chains of fear stopping them from playing, chains of fear around their feet so they won't dance, chains around their neck so they won't sing, chains around their body so they won't marry, chains around their heart so they won't have a baby because they're afraid they won't be a good mother.

The Holy Spirit wants to burn off the chains.

Say this aloud: "Holy Spirit, I receive your fire to burn off any chains or bondages of fear, or chains around my eyes, hands, and ears, all chains that I have experienced and/or allowed. Thank you, Holy Spirit, for setting me free now. And I receive it."

Obedience is Better than Sacrifice

The Holy Spirit had been stirring me to go to Prayer Mountain in Moravian Falls, North Carolina for years, but I couldn't justify the cost of sitting in the woods over there, when I could do that here, camping.

However, God had plans for me to go and he orchestrated it for me to be interviewed by Donna Grisham on the set of It's Supernatural at Sid Roth Studios.

The day after the interview, I discovered that Prayer Mountain was only two hours from my hotel, so early that morning I entered the address on my phone into my GPS and pressed "GO." In case you don't know, GPS is short for Global Positioning System and it gave me the exact arrival time and directions to Prayer Mountain.

With total confidence that GPS knew how to direct me to Prayer Mountain, I started out with my car, following each prompt, each turn, and each light. About one and a half hours into the drive I heard angels ahead of me clapping and shouting, "She's coming, She's coming!" I thought it was odd that they knew I was going to Prayer Mountain.

As GPS led me on the final long and winding one-lane road up the mountain, I began feeling a little anxious.

Thoughts of doubt began to fill my mind, "What if I had put in the wrong destination? I feel like I should be there already. The journey doesn't look like what I thought it would look like. It looks scary..."

So I started to doubt GPS, "Does GPS know what it's doing and where it's taking me? What if I run out of gas? What if GPS stops working because I don't have the internet anymore?" ... I had no choice but to trust GPS's directions and the 'blue line' it showed me as a visual guide.

After winding around the narrow road, up and over the hill, I noticed that I could not even *see* the road ahead of me — if there was any. So, by faith, I just kept driving forward. Then I finally saw the parking lot and arrived at the location — exactly when and where GPS told me I would!

The tiny parking area only allowed space for three to five cars. Letting out a sigh of relief I stopped and got out of the car and began walking along the trail at the top of the mountain. The atmosphere on Prayer Mountain is open, clean, pure, and genuinely unique.

As I walked along I remembered seeing on social media, that people had posted pictures of a small pile of rocks in this area. I was wondering where that stone pile might be located. Then I felt the Holy Spirit leading me to walk over by some trees. I looked down — and there was the little pile of rocks I had been looking for! The stones had names, scriptures, and blessings painted on them. I found another little rock, prayed over it, and placed it on the stones as a memorial.

I thought, "This is a place where God is."

The Holy Spirit often uses the little things to confirm that I am following his lead. When you obey his voice, he will lead you to the place that you have on your heart (from him).

GPS vs. Holy Spirit

As I was praying on the mountain, I heard the name "Bob Jones." I knew the Holy Spirit was directing me to Morning Star to see Bob Jones' Vision Center. So I entered the address into GPS and pressed "GO." GPS told me how to wind down this one-lane road, turning here, and making a sharp turn there … .

It said, "You will arrive at your final destination in twenty miles."

I sat back in faith trusting GPS's voice, and then I heard the Holy Spirit say tenderly, "You have never had lunch with GPS. You have never taken GPS into your prayer room. You have never had a relationship with GPS. GPS has never whispered scriptures of love to you when you were sick, or comforted you when you were in bed. Yet people sit back, have their drinks and eat their snacks mindlessly trusting that GPS will lead them to their final destination. They don't even look at the street signs when GPS tells them to turn. They totally trust GPS."

"I need you to trust in me like you do GPS. I know your final destination. The journey may not look like you thought it would. Sometimes twists and turns may seem scary, but I know your final destination and your exact arrival time — trust Me as you trust GPS."

Trust in the Lord completely, and do not rely on your opinions. With all your heart, rely on him to guide you, and he will lead you in every decision you make. Become intimate with him in whatever you do; he will lead you wherever you go. (Proverbs 3:5- 6 TPT)

"Are not all the angels ministering spirits sent out [by God] to serve (accompany, protect) those who will inherit salvation? [Of course, they are!]" (Hebrews 1:14 AMP)

Be Willing to Move

Sitting in my comfortable chair at the campground this week, a wooden fence-type rail around the campsite blocked me from seeing the lake. I complained even though I still had the ability to walk to the fence, look over, or walk around in order to see the lake if I wanted to. But every time I returned to my comfortable chair I'd complain that it was the fence's fault that I couldn't see the lake clearly.

The Holy Spirit asked, "What blocks people from seeing an open Heaven and gazing on Jesus — when Jesus himself prophesied the truth that we will see an open Heaven?"

My anwer: "We fear what we might see in Heaven."

We fear because maybe we have seen violence, pornography, unclean movies, or we've read stories that have filled our imaginations with impure images. We end up being afraid of what is in our imagination. In that case, we need to ask the Holy Spirit to purge our imagination and sanctify it for him — then we won't have to fear what he might want to show us.

Perhaps we doubt that we have the ability to see because others have told us we cannot or should not be able to see. Or maybe it could be our location: In other words perhaps our church discourages intimate relationships or encounters with Jesus.

The Holy Spirit may want you to move from where you are sitting. I had the whole campground to walk around where I could have seen clearly, but I refused to change my position, because I was comfortable. My camping spot was the best place in the campground and I was proud to be there. But sometimes the best place isn't right, so, we should be willing to move from where we have "camped."

Seeing in the spirit comes from a relationship with the Holy Spirit. It's not head knowledge, it's developed by spending quiet time talking to him, trusting him, trusting his guidance, and learning to hear his voice.

> I prophesy to you eternal truth (there is no lie in him, no hidden motive): From now on, you all will see an open Heaven and gaze (which means to look in admiration) upon the Son of Man like a stairway reaching into the sky with the messengers of God climbing up and down upon him!" (John 1:51 TPT)

> Someone living on an entirely human level rejects the revelations of God's Spirit, for they make no sense to him. He can't understand the revelations of the Spirit because they are only discovered by the illumination of the Spirit. (1 Corinthians 2:14 TPT)

Hormone Disruption and Infertility: It's About the Babies

At 2:00 a.m. the Holy Spirit woke me up to pray. I prayed in the spirit and kept hearing "Hormone Disruption."

Later that morning while in my prayer room I heard the Holy Spirit say, "Hormone disruption is a demonic spirit over the land; this spirit causes female hormones to lower or be restricted causing infertility. It also causes extreme estrogen, which causes seizures and weight gain. These chemicals have been allowed in your fabrics, food, shampoos, cosmetics, and laundry soap. It is sprayed over your land and affects soil, vegetables, schoolyards, crops, cattle, deer, buffalo, fish, and water."

Holy Spirit continued, "This demonic spirit causes infertility and is at the root of the chemicals that have been allowed. Some doctors are banned from checking these hormones, and some labs are prohibited from doing blood work for these hormones. The government knows this and is allowing it to be done. They spray chemicals over the land that have the same ill-effect on animals, bees, birds, and cattle, causing infertility hormones in every species. They know what they are doing, and so do I."

He said, "But I am arresting it today in the highest courts (Heavenly courts). And I am removing from the lower courts (Earthly courts) those that are allowing this. I am ruling that these chemicals are banned from the land! The Supreme Court has looked the other way for too long. I am removing those that are removing my children from being birthed. This is a spirit of abortion. And now I am aborting them from their place of rulership. These chemicals are banned from the land — MY land. People know chemicals are in the foods they eat, but feel they have no choice or voice."

"I say, 'Stand up and fight against this infertility spirit. Stand up and command the Supreme Court to remove these chemicals from the land. They cannot be shipped into this country. No product containing hormone disruption chemicals will be allowed."

In a vision, I saw Jesus as the lion with fire flashing like lightning from his mouth. Then I saw many lions running behind him across the land, with fire flashing from their mouths as well. When God's people (as kings) stand up and roar his words, we become roaring lions.

> The rage of a king is like the roar of a lion, but his sweet
> favor is like a gentle, refreshing rain. (Proverbs 19:12 TPT)

Blade of Fire

After fasting for three days, I heard a roar like a mighty river and felt power flow through me. Then I saw a circular blade made of fire coming at me. It divided me. And then a grey spirit (the spirit of doubt) flew out of me.

I heard, "Divided between soul and spirit. This comes out only by fasting and prayer — not because of such power but because of your place next to Me, because of your confidence, because of you being in the Spirit. This 'doubt if it will work' spirit was hidden deep within you."

Spending time with Jesus and trusting the Holy Spirit's work can deliver you from spirits hidden in your soul.

Chapter Four

Animals

He Loves the Birds

While camping last month, I was getting ready to start working on this book – when the Holy Spirit stopped me.

I heard the Holy Spirit say, "Listen to the birds."

Then in an encounter, I saw Daddy God standing in a flower garden waiting for me in the spirit realm. I went to him. He hugged me and we began walking and holding hands.

He said, "It's not about producing or doing something for me. It's about knowing me." Then he began telling me things about himself.

He said, "I LOVE the birds!" He extended the word "love," for emphasis, everytime he spoke the word.

I said, "Yes, I do too."

Unexpectedly, I felt his overwhelming love for the birds.

He said, "I LOVE the birds." Daddy God held out his finger and a bird flew over and landed on his finger.

He said, "I LOVE their little beaks," and kissed the bird's beak on his finger.

"I LOVE their little feather head," as he petted it.

"I LOVE their feet and how they hold on to me."

"I LOVE their feather wings and design."

"I LOVE how they hover over the water."

"I love birds so much — that's why the Holy Spirit is referred to as a dove."

He said, "In Noah's Ark, a bird brought the answer. With Elijah, birds brought provision. I see when a sparrow falls, and that's not a symbolic statement. It's because I love them so much."

He then said, "There's no bird poop in Heaven," and he laughed.

"You would find Jesus among the flowers, but you will find me among the birds."

I watched Daddy God design the feathers. He was sitting at a table as he began painting a feather. I appeared to be about three years old as I sat down beside him. He put his arm around me and pulled me closer to him so I could watch. He didn't tell me to go away while he was busy creating. And as a child would, I asked questions.

I began asking, "Why, Daddy, are you using that color? Why are you doing that design? Why does the color spiral outwards?"

As an adult I have learned that sometimes artists use different colors with a motive to create an emotion or a certain effect, so I was wondering what his motive was.

He laughed and said, "I don't have a motive. It's who I am. I put into the design of the bird, who I am."

And he puts inside of you and me…. who he is.

> He will cover you and completely protect you with His feathers, And under His wings, you will find refuge; His faithfulness is a shield and a wall. (from Psalm 91:4 AMP)

Dinosaurs

GOD can come to you in a form just so you can have a relationship with him. One day in Heaven the Father (Daddy God) took me by the hand and we walked through a green field.

Daddy God said, "Do you want to see a place I love?"

I said, "Yes."

He took me by the hand, swung me up on top of his shoulders and walked to the edge of a green grassy rolling mountain. Way below us were dinosaurs eating, walking, and playing with each other. We walked down to the green valley and he let me get on a Brontosaurus with a long neck. Other dinosaurs were walking around us. Daddy God rode behind me so I wouldn't be scared. (I still have my soul in these Heavenly encounters, so I remember the feelings I had.)

He said, "I love these that I made."

The revelation I needed to know was that the Father desired to show me something he loves, and that I am always safe with him. I can trust when I'm having fun, and I can trust being with him.

Daddy God has made the way for him to have a relationship with his children.

Wise Talking Horse

I saw Peal (my horse in Heaven) and got on his back. He was so soft and white.

Peal said, "He (Jesus) is not mad at you or upset with you, he is just pruning."

While walking along the river, Peal continued to say, "When you prune and cut back your plants, you don't hate them, you aren't mad at them. You see them and say, 'You'll do better and be healthier if I cut off the dead stuff.'"

"They will, and so will you. You'll look back and say, 'I'm so much better than I used to be.'" Peal stopped walking and we laid down in the soft green grass.

I petted his clean, white mane and coat — they were SO soft — and I said, "Yeah, I just thought I was better than I am."

He laughed and said, "You'll always be improving."

> And we all, with unveiled face, continually seeing as in a mirror the glory of the Lord, are progressively being transformed into His image from [one degree of] glory to [even more] glory, which comes from the Lord, [who is] the Spirit. (2 Corinthians 3:18 AMP)

Riding Fast

Peal, my Heavenly horse, came and said, "I've missed you. Come, we must go fast." As we rode fast, we went through the darkness. I could tell I was glowing with light. I looked at the line of horses beside me and noticed others were riding with me, they were glowing with light too.

We all came to a circular hole, then we circled the hole and looked down through it. In the hole we saw a fire going down to the Earth. We proclaimed the Fire of God to go and purge the country of child perversion.

We proclaimed, "Purge the internet, cell phones, police, fire departments, daycares, and every home of child perversion!"

After a while I saw what looked like veins of fire running through my town: cleaning out, revealing, healing, and bringing repentance. I believe God has great plans for my town and yours, too. So declare the fire of God is cleansing your neighborhood, parks, and city too.

And [the Lord] spoke to the man ·clothed in linen and said, Go in among the whirling wheels under the cherubim; fill your hands with coals of fire from between the cherubim and scatter them over the city. And he went in before my eyes. (Ezekiel 10:2 ESV)

Dog Houses

The dog houses in Heaven are pretty elaborate.

Jesus showed me a dog house that was more like a twenty-story penthouse — just for one labrador. We were suddenly standing inside a room that appeared to be round with glass walls, when a sliding door opened and a labrador came bolting through.

Jesus and I stood to watch this blond lab run up the spiral runway to the top floor, stopping on the upper floor. The top floor had a funnel through which a ball would drop, bounce on a circular bowl like a disc plate, and then bounce randomly so the dog chasing it never knew which way it was bouncing.

The dog then ran to the next floor where there was all kinds of furniture to jump on and run across. He went to the next floor where food was on a long table. He would jump up on a chair and eat the food from the table or stand on the floor and eat from one of the shorter-legged tables.

Then he ran down to the next floor which was filled with children who wanted to play with him. The children would pet, kiss, rub, tickle, and lay on him — of course, he could not get enough attention.

The dog ran down to the next floor where there was a water park with pools to swim in and water squirting up in many places. He could play in the water as long as he wanted. One of the floors had a ball pit where the dog would jump and play, tossing and biting at the balls. Another floor had a tall slide, and this dog loved sliding down it, repeatedly .

I stood next to Jesus as I was watching all this, and said, "This is pretty extreme for a dog, isn't it?"

Jesus leans over to me and says, "It's pretty E-LAB...orate, LAB, LAB-ORATE, pretty elaborate, isn't it?" Then he throws his head back and laughs.

Jesus made a joke, a Dad joke!

Chapter 5

Loved Ones

My Daughter Can Cook

I saw Joy (my daughter in Heaven) today and she said to me, "Mom, we have all of eternity together. I'm so proud of you. You're getting ready to burst forth and change history for many."

"Look Mama, I can cook." I saw a vast banquet table covered with food, and there were many more like it.

Knowing what I was thinking, she laughed and said, "Oh, I didn't cook all this, but I helped. We're getting ready for when you come, for when they come. I can't wait for you to join us. There's so much joy here."

She put a necklace of flowers on my neck (handmade from colorful field flowers) and said, "Listen, they sing."

I Saw My Mom

I saw my mom in a group of people.

She walked up and said, "I'm sorry I made fun of you; I just didn't understand."

Then she flung her arms out wide and said, "But I do now," and everyone laughed!

She pointed to Jesus and said, "Do what He says!" (always a mother)

She hugged me tight and said, "Come look at this."

My mom has a pond in Heaven like she had on Earth in her backyard (except her Earthly fish kept dying). She showed me one huge goldfish, another beautiful blue fish, and then one that turned colors like the rainbow. I cried because I was so happy for her, knowing how much she loved her fish.

She laughed joyfully and said, "He is so good; I wish I would have done more for him while I was there. But you can. Go and tell everyone that this place is real. Tell them Heaven is real, and He is so good."

People in Heaven are free of heaviness and consequently, very happy.

She kissed me on the forehead and said, "It is worth whatever you must do or go through. Keep telling them about this place; it's worth it. Keep doing what He tells you to do."

Jesus said, "This realm is easy; living here is easy. Don't be surprised when you are sent somewhere to minister." He said this with a big grin on his face. This was before the invitations began to come in for me to speak at conferences and on cruises.

...

Later that evening, I was worshipping on earth, and saw a wall around me swirling and forming a whirlwind that went upwards to Heaven.

I heard the Holy Spirit say, "A way has been made for you to enter the Throne Room of God." I began going up and found myself right beside Daddy God. I knelt beside him, put my head onto his lap, and wrapped my arm around his hips.

I didn't see any walls or ceilings in the Throne Room but I turned and saw Mom dancing on the Throne Room floor with little kids laughing and holding balloons; she waved at me. Then she and the kids let go of their balloons and looked up, waving and saying "Bye" to the balloons. I watched Mom playing with the kids, they tickled and climbed all over her while she was lying down, laughing.

Then she got up, blew me a kiss, and said, "I'll see you soon. Do what He says (pointing to God), he knows what he is talking about." She and the kids happily skipped off.

Daddy said, "I am giving you a new layer." I felt a light (not heavy) covering descend on me. And then a refreshing covering flowed over me like a waterfall.

As I sat by Daddy God's throne with my head in his lap, and was watching kids play, dance, and worship him, I thought, "He loves it when his children take the time to be with him."

"MOM, I'm Okay!"

I prayed in tongues for an hour and sang in tongues for almost forty-five minutes. Suddenly, I could feel God's heavy presence in the room. This amount of time isn't always needed to enter into his presence, but this is how today went. The Holy Spirit began using my voice to sing. It was no longer me singing in the spirit but the Holy Spirit singing through me.

At the time I could audibly hear flittering wing tips hitting the ceiling but couldn't see anything in the natural. Suddenly I was in Heaven and saw Daddy God; he hugged me.

Joy (my daughter in Heaven) came up and hugged me and said, "Mom, I'm okay. I'm okay."

Then hundreds of children the age of teenagers appeared to me and said, "Tell our moms we're okay. Will you tell our moms, 'We don't hate them and we are okay?'"

I said to them, "They know that."

They all shook their heads and said, "No, they don't. Tell them we are okay. They don't know. Will you be our voice?"

I said, "Yes, I'll tell them."

A Loved One Passed Away

While sleeping in bed, I was caught up in the spirit to Heaven and saw a relative who passed away the day before. In a bubbly manner, she said happily, "This place is amazing. It's so full of life and joy. Tell my sister I made it."

She lifted her arms, looked down, and said, "I'm beautiful."

She spun around in her beautiful dress and said, "I'm beautiful. Look at my teeth. I'm beautiful! Tell Mom, tell my kids, tell my girls, I will meet them here."

Then she said, "I heard that they are having a party for me (in Heaven)."

As she began to run off, she stopped and said, "Don't stop talking about this place. I'll meet them here, I'll meet them." Then she ran to her party.

Later, I told her mom what I saw and she cried, telling me her daughter had always felt ugly (I never knew).

When you seek Jesus he will sometimes bring loved ones to you to encounter in Heaven. Don't seek people. Seek Jesus. He knows when the time is right.

Seeing My Sister in Heaven

My sister passed away, and I got to see her in Heaven. She did not see Jesus and me as we watched her.

Sitting at a banquet table filled with food, she ate a warm, gooey, caramel apple – and popcorn while laughing and talking to Ruth and Boaz. There were other people at the table but Ruth and Boaz were the ones I could see.

Jesus said, "Kathy is eating a caramel apple with her teeth."

I had forgotten she had dentures (which she would not wear). But she loved caramel apples and popcorn which are hard to eat without teeth.

I saw her again later when Jesus brought her up to me.

She hugged me and said, "Oh, you came to see me!"

She lived out of state and always wanted me to visit her. She took me by the hand and led me to a river where she splashed me. When we were younger we always played in the water. She looked about 20 years old, had all of her teeth, and was totally free from all bondage.

Chapter 6

Angel Encounters

Unseen Stairs

I was reading my Bible and listening to worship music when I stopped and began to turn my mind off the daily events, to focus on Jesus. As I stepped into the spirit realm I was suddenly with a very peaceful, gentle female angel, and we were in her long vehicle riding *over* dirt roads.

While looking at me, she said, "If you don't like going on dirt roads, go above them." And so we rode above the dirt roads, about ten feet off the ground like it was no problem.

Then she started walking up some invisible stairs, and did it so easily.

I asked, "How do you do that?"

She looked puzzled and said, "I just do it." She turned and kept walking upwards. I followed her by walking on the stairs which I could not see, but could still feel under my feet.

I don't recall where we went, but Genesis 28:12 came alive that day. I was amazed at how different life on Earth is compared to living in the spirit realm.

A question is now stirring in me, "Do I have the ability to move in the spirit realm like Jesus?"

> He had a dream of a stairway securely fixed on the Earth and reaching into Heaven. And there were messengers of God ascending and descending on the stairway. (Genesis 28:12 TPT)

I Could Watch Myself

I was worshipping when I saw Daddy God. He hugged me, and we sat on a swing in the front porch of a house in Heaven.

He said, "I always sat with you on the front porch of your house when you were growing up. That's why you enjoy this."

...

Then I saw an angel and knew she was there to show me around. She was lovely and covered in jewels. We walked past something like a glass wall where we could see what was taking place on the earth; we saw demonic beings.

She said, "These we will deal with later, but not right now."

Then I saw a sizeable demonic being (almost like a movie-sized alligator), lying down and protecting eggs.

She said, "This demonic being guards family generations from becoming all they are to be."

...

Then she took me by the hand and introduced me to a younger angel named Sally, who appeared to be jovial and wanted to play.

She said, "Ok, first thing, you have to relax. Don't try to figure it out with your head. Relax, take a deep breath, and relax." So I did.

We got in what looked like a coal miner's car. We rode through a tunnel, got out and went up some stairs. And now I was "watching" myself doing this.

She said, "You are in the Father. And he is in you, and watching you at all times — so you are watching you at all times."

We walked across a wooden walkway, climbed over some hurdles, and rolled through some doors. She laughed at the fact that I would turn and look at her. I was watching her because the Father was watching me, and I was in him.

She laughed and said, "This is very important for you to know. You now have more eyes — eyes to see what you are doing at all times."

Then I was back with Daddy who said, "You can come to me so easily at any time."

I'm watching myself as I write this but I don't know why. Knowing I'm in the Father and he is in me, I can always see myself, and so can he, because we are one.

The next day I watched myself all day, like in the third person and knew how I felt about everything and knew every thought I was thinking. I noticed that I'm always focused on God in everything I do. It was so encouraging to know my heart is fixed on him.

> For in Him we live and move and exist [that is, in Him, we actually have our being], as even some of your poets have said, 'For we also are His children.' (Acts 17:28 AMP)

Angel Named Prosperity

Early in the morning, I prayed and sang Revelation 4:3 about seeing the colors around the Throne. It's good to sing the Bible in whatever tune comes to you. Doing this helps to get the scriptures in your spirit, not just your head.

> Speak to one another in psalms and hymns and spiritual songs, [offering praise by] singing and making melody with your heart to the Lord; (Ephesians 5:19 AMP)

After singing the scripture, suddenly I could see Jesus sitting with swirls of thick colors around him. They were the deepest reds, purples, and blues. Then an angel named Prosperity stood beside me. He looked like he had the Lord's colors in his wings and body too, but they kept changing.

Daddy said, "I made this angel, Prosperity, with the Lord's colors."

I invited the angel into the ministry that the Father has given to me. Then I realized I was standing in Jesus by his throne.

Jesus said, "I can give you more power and authority because you stand in My love. You will know My love, so you will respond with My love when you operate in My authority and power. I know you, and you know and have My heart and my love. I give you power and authority."

I watched as the colors swirled around.

> Are not all the angels ministering spirits sent out [by God] to serve (accompany, protect) those who will inherit salvation? [Of course they are!] (Hebrews 1:14 AMP)

Angel Eyes and Angel of Lightning

I got up at 7:00 am to pray and listen to John Tussey's Frequencies of Thought. Once again in Heaven, Jesus and I danced. Today, it was on ice. As one, we were beautifully flowing on the ice, just like in the Olympics. He wore pants with material that flowed as he skated, and I wore light-flowing fabrics.

I saw an angel on the ice. The angel raised his wings and stretched them out. His wings looked like the designs of peacock feathers with eyes inside and outside of the wings.

As the angel spun around with his wings stretched out, I heard, "Eyes within, eyes around."

Then I saw another angel. He seemed to be made of lightning.

He came to dance with me and said, "I am made by your Father, so don't be afraid to dance with me."

Lightning shot out of his face, ears, and arms; every part of him had lightning shooting outwards as he danced. The lightning bent and flowed with his rhythm. I skated up to him, and then the lightning angel wrapped his wings around me.

He said, "Flow with love. Don't look at the lightning strikes, but flow with love."

I felt his name was Angel Strikes. It is not like an angel would strike with lightning to hurt someone, but speaking God's words with love brings these strikes of lightning — which brings change and penetrates even a hardened heart.

Later, as I sat at my kitchen table remembering Angel Strikes, he came walking into my kitchen and sat at the table across from me! Angel Strikes was just sitting there looking at me, smiling, with lightning shooting from his face, neck, shoulders, and chest.

He smiled and said, "Don't seek the lighting, seek his (Jesus') voice. The lightning is a fruit." Then suddenly, he was gone.

> And the four living creatures, each one of them having six wings, are full of eyes around and within; and day and night they do not cease to say, "HOLY, HOLY, HOLY IS

THE LORD GOD, THE ALMIGHTY, WHO WAS AND WHO IS AND WHO IS TO COME (Revelation 4:8 AMP)

His body also was like beryl [with a golden luster], his face had the appearance of lightning, his eyes were like flaming torches, his arms and his feet like the gleam of burnished bronze, and the sound of his words was like the noise of a multitude [of people or the roaring of the sea]. (Daniel 10:6 AMP)

The angel's appearance was like lightning, and his clothes were as white as snow. (Matthew 28:3 AMP)

The voice of the Lord strikes with flashes of lightning. (Psalm 29:7-11 NIV)

Angels at Angel Cabin

I was invited to speak at a women's conference on Prayer Mountain at Apple Hill Lodge in Moravian Falls, North Carolina.

On the very first day, in a cabin called, "Angel Cabin," I noticed the presence of God was really heavy. I sat on the couch with my eyes closed, enjoying his presence, wondering what the angels would look like. When I opened my eyes I saw in the spirit realm (not in the natural as I would see you), four angels were bending over and looking at me.

I thought, "What are they looking at?"

One of the angels said, "We want to see what you look like!" I thought that was funny because we want to know what they look like. They took on the appearance of humans; they were dressed in robes and I could tell they had wings.

One of the ladies staying in the cabin with us, walked in and said, "Wow, the presence is so heavy." Slowly, she sank behind the chair because of God's heavy presence. Then the angels were gone.

The second night, I was in bed when I heard what sounded like a group of people, maybe six or so, moving around in the kitchen and living room (I knew they were angels). I listened as they walked around, it sounded like they were packed in the house. I could hear as their wings were rubbing against each other. They walked up and down the stairs and I also heard them walking on the roof. One of the ladies heard them and went outside in the dark to see if a tree was hitting the roof, causing noise. But no tree was touching the roof.

The last night in the cabin I was alone. I heard heavy footsteps outside my window. At first it sounded like someone was walking on the gravel road, which was about ten feet away from the house, and about a seven-foot drop below the house. Next I noticed that the sound was right beside the bedroom window. Then I heard an angel walk behind my room, and suddenly he stood beside my bed. I didn't open my eyes because I could see the angel with my eyes closed.

This angel gently laid a blanket over me like a mother would a sleeping child and said, "I cover you with the blessings from your Father. He is very pleased with you!" Suddenly, the angel was gone.

Angels at Apple Hill Lodge

By the conference room at Apple Hill Lodge in Moravian Falls, before the meeting started, I looked out the window and saw about five young angels playing tag around the gazebo. They looked like young teenage boys, except they had wings and wore robes. They were chasing each other and laughing.

At the same time I saw another young angel swinging from under the wooden staircase like you might swing from monkey bars on a playground.

Not all angels are tall, older, military, in full armor, and ready to battle — some play and have fun. I knew that some angels liked to have fun because of my angel called Entertaining Angel, who I wrote about in my book *Heaven is Real and FUN*. He makes me laugh when he shows up.

Angel Learning to Ride

Later, when Kelsey, Rick, and I returned to Prayer Mountain, I saw a young angel with wings who looked like he was riding on a tree which was leaning way over. He was riding the tree like a child would pretend to be riding a horse.

I asked Jesus, "Why?"

Jesus said, "He is practicing riding a horse because he will be in the Army of the Lord."

Angels with Spines

While praying, I saw angels standing straight, almost in military style, and each one held a spine. Ther angels looked human-like but were much taller and more muscular. They stood spine in hand, like they were on a mission (they did not look very joyful). Then I saw one walk in front of a person needing a spine, and I heard myself count to three out loud. When I said "three," the angel thrust the spine through the person's chest, let it go inside the person and then pulled their empty hand out!

In my first book (in chapter 1) I described seeing body parts in Heaven. The Body Parts Storehouse in Heaven has every body part that you could need on Earth.

"Are not all the angels ministering spirits sent out [by God] to serve those who will inherit salvation?" (Hebrews 1:14 AMP)

Encounter with Native Angels

I heard the beating of many drums surrounding us. The deep, cadence of the drums (slow enough to make white people dance, LOL) is a call to the Native Angels. Then I saw a jungle with native-looking angels approaching, dressed for battle. They were wild-haired, big and rugged looking like a native warrior might look. They had a no-nonsense style, very fierce and intentional.

They were being called to rescue those who were captured, and to return them to their original design (creative miracles). They were being called to rescue those who have been taken captive by the "transgender, sexually-perverted enemy."

The Native Angels are being called to restore people to their native or original design. So people *will be* restored to their original design.

Encounter with Sheep Shearing Angel

An angel was suddenly standing in front of my desk. He was very straight and strong. He was coming for instructions and then waiting to be released. I began commanding him to do this and that, but he stood there, not moving.

So I asked him, "What is your name? Why are you here? What is your purpose?" (because obviously, what I'd said wasn't right).

He pulled out a sharp blade that looked like a long ice scraper and said, "I'm here to shear the sheep!"

I thought, "Oh, that can't be good."

He said, "I'm here to cut away the matted wool from around the sheep's eyes that keep them closed. I'm here to cut the mats from the sheep's ears so they can hear clearly. I'm here to cut and skillfully remove the mats weighing down the sheep, so they are free of the heaviness they have been carrying around. I'm here to open the eyes of the sheep."

He showed me how he skillfully cuts away the heavy, matted hair from the eyes of the sheep, so now they can see!

Angel of Peace

At Prayer Mountain in Moravian Falls, North Carolina, as I walked along the top ridge of the mountain and sat beside a tree, I saw two angels standing beside another tree.

One dressed in a white robe with deep pink trim, turned and said, "Shhh," to the other angel who was talking to her.

"Shhh, she's receiving Peace."

She smiled at me and said, "Shhh, quiet your mind and listen."

Then she asked, "What do you see?"

I got quiet and looked (you don't see if you don't look), I saw the lower leaves gently blowing in a tiny breeze. Then I could feel this tiny breeze.

Holy Spirit said, "You would have missed the blowing breeze because you are so busy. Always going and moving in a rush, you miss the gentleness of my breeze. My leading is a gentle breeze, a whisper, the slightest nudge. But while you are going and rushing, you pass by the moment and it is gone. The encounter is missed. Soft, tender leaves feel the slightest breeze."

The angel turned to me and said, "Don't be in a hurry to go."

I felt sleepy but the Holy Spirit said, "When you or someone else feels peace and safety, they can sleep."

I understand people have difficulty sleeping because they don't feel at peace or safe.

> In peace [and with a tranquil heart] I will both lie down and sleep, For You alone, O Lord, make me dwell in safety and confident trust. (Psalm 4:8 AMP)

Angels of Oil

Later that day I was lying on my bed resting when I saw the Holy Spirit and three angels standing at the end of my bed. The angels were pouring oil over me.

The Holy Spirit said, "We are infilling you with My presence. People are coming to encounter Me, to seek My presence, and an encounter with Me. I am pouring into you so you can pour into them."

Chapter 7

Other Encounters

Wooden Porch and Chair

I was caught up into Heaven and sat in an oversized wooden chair that was on an old wooden porch. I was beside an elderly lady, and looking over at her, I recognized that this was Ruth from the Bible. I had seen her in Heaven before, she has a grandma type of sweetness about her.

Leaning my head on her shoulder, she had her arm around me and said, "Tell me what's bothering you." I began to cry and tell her all the things that were bothering me at that time.

She said, "It's all going to be OK."

Later that day my husband and I walked around downtown. We saw a small, old-looking building, and as I approached it I noticed it had an old wooden porch with an old wooden chair much like the one I'd seen in Heaven.

I heard Jesus say, "This is to let you know that what you saw was real."

When you have encounters in Heaven, you still have your soul and you remember things from the Earth. Jesus wants you to step into Heaven to release your burdens and heal your heart.

In 2/23/2012, I was Commissioned

Bill Johnson:

I was attending a meeting with Bill Johnson, Tom Jones, and Randy Clark.

Bill Johnson said, "I impart the healing anointing on people called into the healing ministry."

He said, "You can know if this is the ministry to which you have been called if you cry, feel heat in your hands, get sweaty hands, or your heart pounds." Well, my hands were sweaty and hot, and I couldn't stop crying, my lips also tingled and vibrated.

Randy Clark:

When Randy laid hands on me, I got very hot.

He said, "Jesus give her love. I release a healing anointing and supernatural miracles." I stood, cried, and shook.

Tom Jones:

Tom prayed this over me, "God fill her up to her capacity, then enlarge her capacity. God, what you did to me, do the same for Kim. She will see the root causes and won't have to search for the cause. Kim, I commission you this day into your destiny in the healing ministry. Fill her hunger. All fear of anything holding her back is gone. Will you wake her up and shake her in the middle of the night?"

And I recalled that a shaking happened to me a few nights earlier.

Jesus said, "You have walked through the veil. You have crossed over and will never be the same."

Court Room

I sat on a red throne in Heaven, taking authority over my town's water supply and parks. From the red throne I spoke purity to the water, declaring my town a place for Christian speakers, and healing, etc. Then I walked into a courtroom in Heaven and sat on the right side in the back.

People said, "Yay, come on in and sit here. The new ones get to watch and learn." The court is lower in the center, and the rows of seats are higher, circling the court like a college professor's lecture class.

Later during prayer, I went to a relative's house (in the spirit), surrounded her property and proclaimed, "A canopy of God's provision, with no backlash after hosting a Christian wedding!"

I declared, "Angels go out to triple their business' income."

She told me later they had so many customers that week that it was like windows of blessings opened above them.

> But in that coming day, no weapon turned against you shall succeed, and you will have justice against every courtroom lie. This is the heritage of the servants of the Lord. This is the blessing I have given you, says the Lord. (Isaiah 54:17 TLB)

Flight of 746

During prayer, I immediately saw a man, a golfer, standing on the edge of a hill in Hawaii. And I noticed there were other men and women present as well, who looked as concerned as I was. We all just suddenly appeared together, looking around at each other knowing we didn't know each other or why we were standing there. The golfer had called us all together.

He said, "I have called you because you want to travel in time, right?"

We all nodded our heads, "Oh yes."

He pointed to me and said, "I know you want heat. I will send you to warm places like Hawaii, Honolulu, and the Caribbean." (Note that at the time this book was written I had not yet been asked to speak in the Caribbean, but since then I have received two invitations to speak on two different cruises to warm places.)

He pointed to the others, saying, "You like the mountains and snow. And you like water … ."

He said, "When you get there, you will minister. Jesus will give you directions, counsel, help, or words of encouragement for the people."

Then I asked, in a thought, "Who are you? A golfer I don't know?"

Just then he turned into Enoch, who had long white hair and a gown-like thing on. I knew it was Enoch even though I had never met him before.

He said, "You will also change appearance depending on the person to whom you minister. Remember when Jesus walked with his very own disciples all day, they didn't even recognize him? And then he turned into Jesus, the one they knew? You will do the same."

He laughed and said, "We need a name for our group. Let's call us the "Flight of 746."

After digging and praying about the number '746' — I found that '7' represents God's perfections, completion, and rest (Genesis 2:2), as well as the gifts of the Spirit. The number '4' Represents God's Path, creative in nature, and the works of God (Genesis 1:1). And '6' represents man: God loves man so much He sent Jesus and the Holy Spirit for them. (Genesis 1:27)

And not only that, a friend noticed that the numbers 7+4+6 equal 17, and gleaned from *biblicalchronology.com* that '17' in the Bible represents "completeness, spiritual renewal, and victory over challenges, symbolizing divine purpose in believers' lives."

So then, "746" would speak of us resting in God's path and trusting his love for those to whom he is sending us, knowing he will release whatever gifts, directions, or encouragements are needed when we get there. It will be his divine purpose for us, and we will have victory over challenges!"

> While they were talking and discussing it, Jesus Himself came up and began walking with them. 16 But their eyes were [miraculously] prevented from recognizing Him. (Luke 24:15-16 AMP)

Ezekiel

This morning Ezekiel and I were together in the spirit.

He said, "You will see lots of things that are hard, or different and difficult to describe to people. When I lay on the ground in my time on Earth, my friends mocked me, spit on me, threw rocks, and kicked dirt at me. I understand being disappointed and betrayed."

He said, "My wife who knew me, didn't 100% totally accept what I was to do, or why, or who I was. I was alone … but not alone."

Ezekiel continued, "As you walk arm in arm with Jesus, obeying him, living by his rules and commands which he gives you today—you'll live well and your children will follow after you." I thanked Ezekiel for speaking to me, and thanked Daddy for allowing him to.

I then sat on my throne over my city and proclaimed from all four corners: "Fire from the river, go to purify this town. And oil of the Holy Spirit, come to pour over this town."

Elijah and the Book

During prayer I saw a bench big enough to seat two people. It had two trees on either side that looked like weeping willows, with long limbs that hung low and swayed gently in the breeze.

A spring or brook ran in front of the bench. The grass was deep green and gently rolled over the edge making a thick, lush border along the water. The edge didn't drop off like a cliff but was like a soft, gentle ramp down to the water. The water was alive, sparkling and fizzy like a soda drink, thick and dense like slick baby oil. Little fish were jumping and swimming in it.

Someone was sitting on the bench holding a book, so I went and sat next to him.

I introduced myself and said, "Hi, I'm Kim."

He said, "Hi, I'm Elijah."

He laughed and I thought for a moment, "Elijah … man, he looks so young and lively!"

I asked, "Elijah, as in THE Elijah?"

He laughed again and said, "As in THE Elijah." But it still didn't register who I was speaking to, I was so focused on the book he was holding.

He was holding the book and turning what looked like pages. But when he turned the pages, I noticed that the images in it were alive! I could see a person's entire life playing like a 3-D video, from the left side of the book to the right side.

For example, I saw airplanes flying, pets running, people walking, trees moving, houses lived in, buildings worked in — all from one person's life. I could see from the beginning, to the middle, to the end. I could even enter the book and observe their life at any point in time!

I tried to discover the name of the person whose story I was seeing but was told, "The 'who' isn't essential, look at the book."

Elijah said, "The best people can do on Earth is write words on paper or make a 3-D pop-up like book — but this is a living book."

He put the book partly in my lap so I could examine it. I turned a page and when I held it to eye level the 'page' looked transparent. But I could see things like they were real, the buildings and people, the horses running, and whatever else was happening in the person's life.

Well, now I wanted to see MY page!

I brought the book fully over to my lap and asked to see my pages. I turned the page and saw myself as a baby, with many red clothes and a very large lake.

Elijah said, "There's lots of water in your life."

I laughed and said, "Yes, I like water."

I saw in the book the time when I was about seven years old when I was brushing my thoroughbred quarter horse (who we did not have for long because we didn't know how to take care of him. I'm hoping I get to see this horse again one day in Heaven). I also saw myself water skiing and snow skiing ... and I even saw myself riding my motorcycle.

As I sat on the bench enjoying my "pages," then I looked up at the green grass across the brook from us. Elijah, who was still sitting beside me, waved his hand.

He thought, (but I could actually hear him as if he spoke out loud), "You like flowers." And instantly, yellow flowers filled the field. He waved his hand back and the flowers turned half red; each flower was half red and half yellow. Then he rubbed his fingers together and purple flowers popped throughout the field.

It was so amazing to me as I sat there, looking at the flowers and holding this fantastic book of life that gave me the ability to enter into a person's life at any point, at any day, hour, moment, or second.

Then, seeing the brook flowing before us, the thought hit me and I said, "The brook — you're ELIJAH AT THE BROOK!" He laughed and was almost as shocked as I was at the revelation.

Putting his hand on his chest, acting surprised at who he was, he said, "Yes, Elijah at the brook." (1 Kings 17:2)

I said, "Elijah at the brook."

He said, "Elijah at the brook," and laughed. We thought it was so funny!

Then he got up and walked over to the brook. It appeared to be shallow enough to walk across. He sat on the edge and dangled his feet in the cool brook. I sat next to him and put my feet in too. We watched little fish swim and jump.

Elijah said, "This isn't like the brook I was at." Then he slid into the water as he held onto the soft green edge, it reached chest deep. When I slid in, the water was up to my chest too. The depth of the brook's water seemed to adjust to the depth each person needed. It was incredible, refreshing, and alive, but I didn't feel wet. I looked over at the trees beside the bench, and noticed how alive they were. Each leaf actually had eyes that watched us. And each tree had a mouth and eyes on its trunk too.

Then my thoughts went to the desires I have; I'm always wanting a word of knowledge or prophetic word for people when I minister to them, and I realized, "Hey, when I'm speaking a word of knowledge, it is like I've actually been holding this live book and sticking my finger into one tiny day, one little hour, one tiny minute of a person's life, and then telling that person about what I was seeing in their life!"

This Heavenly knowledge would bring so much encouragement to the person I was ministering to, to let them know that God really cares about what they have been through. When I partner with the Holy Spirit, Who is the Spirit of Knowledge, I should be able to see any portion of a person's life, from beginning to end. So I prayed for an increase of knowledge and faith to see the whole picture, in order to be the blessing God wants me to be for them.

After this encounter, I realized we have been given the Spirit of knowledge, which is the Holy Spirit. He is living in us so we can press into the Holy Spirit and partner with him for much more than what we've already experienced.

> 'Call to Me and I will answer you, and tell you [and even show you] great and mighty things, [things which have been confined and hidden], which you do not know and understand and cannot distinguish.' (Jeremiah 33:3 AMP)

Woodworking Shop in a Mansion

Jesus has shown me a woodworking shop the size of a warehouse, as part of someone's mansion in Heaven. Woodworking shops are there for both men and women. One women's workshop, which I saw, had more plants in it than the man's shop that I was taken to:

This man's woodworking shop was filled with every kind of machine: sanders, routers, drills, etc., and even other machines that hadn't been invented yet on Earth. And note, there was no sawdust to clean up.

The shop didn't have a ceiling so there was a lot of natural light (but there were no bugs, thieves, or rain to deal with). One neat thing was that the machines would move towards the person when they needed it; the person didn't have to walk over to each of the different machines every time they worked on one piece of wood.

"And no cussing or auguring would be here," Jesus said.

The shop also had a movie studio with chairs that conform to your body, with food and drinks instantly appearing. In addition, the walls of the shop were like giant TV screens. Every kind of sport, including airplane races, fishing, bike races, snow and water-skiing, horse races, westerns and more, could be watched.

And because the TV screen is a portal, anyone in the shop, when they wanted, could step through it and immediately be in a bike race, a fishing boat, or riding a horse in a Western movie to arrest the bad guys. Then, in an instant they could step back into the shop.

I saw families making wooden furniture, working together as they did on the Earth in their family business. And when someone wanted a piece of furniture, they just gave it away — no taxes. Everything is free because Jesus has paid for it all.

I also saw that fathers could work with their sons and daughters, teaching them how to make things, even though they hadn't gotten the opportunity to do so on Earth.

In the workshop I saw a man stop and then begin to worship the Father; he was so thankful for what the Father had made for him. He was overwhelmed with thankfulness and love for the Father, he felt so loved by Jesus' generosity to him. I watched this man step through a portal and appear instantly in the Throne Room to worship the Father.

Then I saw someone who I did not know, but I understood that they were once in a wheelchair on the Earth, and now they were walking into their workshop. They were healed, energized, smiling, and so happy.

Jesus will restore everything!

> Return to your rest, O my soul, For the Lord has dealt bountifully with you. (Psalm 116:7)

Chapter 8

The Circus in Heaven

The Circus in Heaven is for the Children

We have a circus on Earth because they first had one in Heaven.

Jesus said, "The circus in Heaven is for the children. Some that have arrived in Heaven never had the opportunity to see or participate in a circus. The child you lost, the grandchildren you didn't get to take to the circus, all of that is restored in Heaven."

Jesus took me to the circus in Heaven for three (Earth) days to reveal his love for the children, and also because Jesus and I are friends. Every time I prayed during those three days, Jesus and I were instantly at the circus. And Even though this experience was separated into three Earth days, it was actually just one long encounter.

I saw a circus tent with flags waving on top of it, and two adult women were walking toward the entryway. As they stepped through the door into the circus, one of the women remained an adult, and the other became a little child. The child took hold of her mother's hand as they smiled, and then mother and daughter sat in the stands to watch the circus.

Then I saw a man and a woman walk up to the tent door. As soon as they crossed over, the man remained a man, but the woman became a little girl and took her dad's hand. Later as they left, holding hands, they stepped out through the tent threshold, and the child became an adult again. They laughed and cheered as they experienced this event together.

Ellie the Elephant

Suddenly, I was riding on the neck of a large elephant with big floppy ears that flapped back and forth, her name was Ellie. I rode her around the circus ring. She would walk on her back two legs as the children cheered. There was a cup-type thing on Ellie's head that I put my head on, to do the headstand as she trotted around the circus ring. The children clapped and cheered as Ellie and I came slowly past them.

Then, lots of big floppy-ear elephants came out into the circus and would bend down so the children could ride them. Since there is no time in Heaven, the children could ride the elephants around the ring and play with them until they were fully satisfied.

I saw children dressed as little ballerinas with ballet shoes and frilly dresses, riding Ellie and doing pirouettes (spinning on one foot) on her head as she walked around. The children also took turns doing headstands on Ellie and on the other elephants.

High-Flying Trapeze

Jesus and I played on the High-Flying Trapeze. Jesus went first while I stood on a small platform on the other side and watched him swing back and forth. He hung upside down from the bar with his knees curled over it, and called for me to jump to him. I was not sure I wanted to do that.

He said, "I'll catch you."

As he swung closer, I jumped, and he grabbed both of my wrists firmly. We swung back and forth and I heard the children cheering for us. Jesus swung me up high in the air, then I spun around and gripped my bar, and swung back to my platform while Jesus landed on his platform on the other side.

Now it was his turn for me to grab his arms. As I swung closer towards Jesus, he exhaled a deep breath and slowly tapped the platform with his toes to see if it was strong enough to hold him … he put his fingers to his mouth and looked upward for help… .

The children below shouted, "You can do it! It's okay, try it!" as they watched intently and cheered for him.

Jesus looked at me with a twinkle, letting me know he was doing an act for the children as I kept swinging back and forth, waiting for him. Then he jumped — and I caught him by one wrist. He acted like he was going to fall. Flinging his arm and legs around, the children gasped with excitement! I then caught his other wrist, and we swung back and forth. The children cheered and applauded for Jesus.

We did flips in the air and then fell into the safety net below, and then bounced up high. And then we flipped back and forth before taking hold of the net's edge, and finally spun over and off.

After landing, we both struck a pose and the children clapped and cheered for us. Jesus beamed with love as the children were so happy with the entertainment.

Lions

I was in the ring as many lions came running out. They had long manes. The lions and I could talk to each other so I told them to jump through the fiery ring that I held, and they would roar. The sound of their roaring filled the tent. The children gasped at their sound and watched as the large lions jumped through the fiery hoop I held (I didn't get burned). The lions jumped quickly one after the other. Then they ran from one platform to the next, and around the ring, as I held the fiery hoop.

One large lion jumped into the center ring with me and stood on his back legs. He put his giant paws on my shoulders. My head measured to the middle of his chest, that's how big he was. Then slow music began to play, and the large lion and I danced together. The children gasped and awed at us. During this lion performance, Jesus sat in the stands with the children to watch with them.

There is no time (or rushing) in Heaven — so at the end of the lion show, all the lions walked up to the side of the bleachers and laid down to let the children lay on them, pet them, kiss them, and ride on them.

The Birds

Then doves and other birds flew into sight. They flew around and landed all over me as I stood in the circus ring. The doves flew into a large box in the center of the ring, not all at once, but taking turns, several at a a time, almost like birds at a bird bath. And with their beaks, they each picked up a small wrapped gift. Then the doves flew over to the children and dropped a small wrapped gift into each child's lap.

As the small children tore away at the ribbons and wrapping paper, they cheered, clapped, and laughed. They hugged and then shook their presents because each was a small snow globe with a LIVE circus inside. When I looked closely at the snow globes, I saw live animals reenacting the circus. The birds landed on the children's shoulders, heads, and legs, and allowed the children to pet, kiss, and hold them (ps. there is no bird poop or trash in Heaven).

Gorilla and Monkeys

A large gorilla came into the ring, lumbered over to me and gave me a big hug. The children "awww-ed" our hug. Then the gorilla picked me up and held me in its hairy arm like I was a baby. The children were overwhelmed as he rocked me repeatedly and touched my nose with his giant monkey finger.

Then hundreds of small monkeys came running out and ran up into the stands where Jesus and the children were. The monkeys crawled up into each child's lap so they could be held, rocked, and played with during the circus. The monkeys would also run behind the children, tickle them, and then run away. They'd mess up the child's hair, or just sit on their heads or shoulders. The children were never afraid but were so excited and happy.

Bike Cage

The next moment I was sitting in the stands with Jesus, eating popcorn and watching the circus. They out-rolled a sizeable, round, wire cage and a person began riding a regular bicycle very low inside the wire cage. As they went faster, they began riding up the sides of the cage.

The children cheered as the rider went around and upside down in the cage; they gasped as they watched the bicycle rider go so fast. As the children left the circus, each one received a brand-new bike.

Jesus said, "People in Heaven teach the ones who never had a bike, how to ride a real bike, like they would have done on Earth. The teachers might be their parents or other family members in Heaven, or even someone who never had a child."

He continued, "If a child wanted to ride in the wire cage, they would be taught how to do it. Then they might ride in the circus in Heaven, or just ride in the cage because they wanted to."

Food at the Circus

Jesus and I were sitting in the stands eating a warm caramel apple; the caramel was still runny, and delicious. I could turn the apple to let the warm caramel slowly coat the other side. Then we ate snow cones made of natural snow and cotton candy; they were made of such bright colors and were so full of flavor.

The children were eating while watching the circus as well. They also had warm caramel apples, cotton candy, and glow stick necklaces. (There's no weight gain in Heaven, no cavities, no food allergies, and no diabetes.)

At the end of the circus the children could go hop on the safety net, do flips, and swing from the lowered trapeze bars if they wanted.

All is Restored in Heaven

We can release all the condemnation, all the guilt, all this disappointment, and all the shame for not taking, or not making the opportunity to take our children to the circus. We'll have lots of opportunities, over and over again, to do just that in Heaven. The child you lost, the grandchildren you didn't get to see — well in Heaven, all of those opportunities to do things with them, are restored.

I noticed that during this circus visit in Heaven, Jesus never referred to children as "kids" — I wondered why.

> … No eye has seen, no ear has heard, and no human mind has conceived the things God has prepared for those who love Him. These are the things God has revealed to us by His Spirit. The Spirit searches all things, even the deep things of God. (from 1 Corinthians 2:9-10 AMP)

> "Pray, then, in this way: 'Our Father, who is in Heaven, Hallowed be Your name. Your kingdom come, Your will be done on Earth as it is in Heaven." (Matthew 6:9 AMP)

Chapter 9

Having Fun with Jesus

Swingy Thingy

While worshipping, I was taken somewhere with Jesus, and we played on this hool-a-hoop type of circle that could spin and swing back and forth. This "toy" had not yet been invented on Earth. It is designed so that you can put your body and arms through the center of the hoop, brace yourself up on the ring with your elbows and arms, and then lift your feet while you then could leave your legs dangling.

Jesus and I laughed as we began spinning around in circles, and were swinging high, with our legs dangling down. Jesus is so fun to play with! He will show you things in Heaven that have not been invented so you can invent them on Earth if you want.

> But just as it is written [in Scripture], "Things which the eye has not seen and the ear has not heard, And which have not entered the heart of man, All THAT, God has prepared for those who love Him [who hold Him in affectionate reverence, who obey Him, and who gratefully recognize the benefits that He has bestowed]." (1 Corinthians 2:9 AMP)

Swimming with the Dolphins

During worship, Jesus said to me, "I love to swim with the dolphins in the pure sea." And then we were instantly in the deep sea, swimming.

A dolphin came by and we held onto its fin. The dolphin dove deeper into the sea that sparkles with life. I noticed I could easily breathe under the water. Yes, in Heaven you can breathe underwater! After a bit, Jesus and I reached up to the top of the pure, sparkling sea.

We began to walk on top of the water, and we were not sinking! The sea is so pure and full of life, it made me cry. Things in Heaven are so overwhelming and wonderful.

I love encounters like these. When life is hard and heavy with decisions, Jesus wants us to be with him to get refreshed and renewed, to be able to love, and live free of the world's ways.

> Set your mind and keep focused habitually on the things above [the Heavenly things], not on things that are on the Earth [which have only temporal value]. 3 For you died [to this world], and your [new, real] life is hidden with Christ in God. (Colossians 3:2-3 AMP)

Sliding Across the Floors

During worship, I saw a long hallway in Heaven with shiny floors, and Jesus was standing at the end of the hallway. He smiled and nodded, knowing I really wanted to slide across the glossy floor. Jesus laughed with me as I slid down the long hallway. It was fun!

Skipping Rocks

I saw Jesus skipping little round rocks.

I asked him, "Why?"

He said, "I like to ... the ones with rough edges don't skip well. But the ones where the edges have been smoothed skip farther, jump well, and go faster to the place where they are to be." He smiled and had a twinkle in his eye.

I knew that was a parable about me (and maybe you). Jesus was telling me I was rough around the edges, but as he smooths off those rough edges, I will travel farther and faster. Once Jesus has smoothed the rough edges off of us, he'll be able to "skip" us and get us to where we are going faster than if we still had our rough edges, or our hard hearts.

> I will give you a new, undivided heart, and I will put a new spirit in you. I will remove your stubborn heart of stone and give you a tender heart that responds to me—a devoted heart. (Ezekiel 11:19 TPT)

Dancing with Jesus

While listening to a soaking CD of John Tussey's called Path of New Beginnings, I visited Jesus. Then Jesus and I danced like we never danced before. He was dressed in a long, flowing robe of gold, and I had on a long robe of white, light-but-thick, soft and fuzzy, material. We danced ballroom style.

Then we began to mesh into each other while we danced and twirled around in the air like the seeds from a maple tree. (As a child, I referred to them as airplane seeds). Jesus and I twirled and danced as one, he in his gold robe and me in my white robe. As our faces came together, we appeared as if we were one. Our robes stretched out as we twirled and danced up in the air through space ... twirling around and around. Near us there were flower peddles falling and singing, and then raindrops were coming down and singing too. Jesus and I were one: face to face, arm in arm, body in body.

Jesus said, "I have made this day for us. You were a spirit before you were a body and we even danced together before you were a body."

> So when that day comes, you will know that I am living in the Father and that you are one with me, for I will be living in you. (John 14:20 TPT)

Bumper Cars and Cotton Candy

I saw the brightest lights; they were even more colorful than the last time Jesus took me to the amusement park. Jesus hugged me, took me by the hand, and handed me a big blue and pink cotton candy.

Jesus said, "I love how it melts in my mouth, turns my fingers different colors, and makes them stick together." And he laughed.

Jesus showed me his sticky fingers and said, "It is not made of sugar, but of light." It was swirling, moving light; you could eat the light, and it really tasted like cotton candy.

He said, "I want to show you a new place at the amusement park that you haven't seen." And then he took me to the bumper cars. My first reaction was dread. As a child I loved driving bumper cars and hitting others, and then getting hit. But as I grew older it began to hurt. That's why, when I saw the bumper cars, I remembered the pain.

One reason Jesus wants you to encounter Heaven is so that he can heal the memories of what caused you pain, and replace them with thoughts of joy.

These cars didn't just stay on the ground though, they went around in a circle up off the ground. And then when I bumped someone, my car would turn colors. I soon realized the object was to bump five cars so that my car could turn purple. Your bumper car could also drop down below your opponent. I tried to bump Jesus' car, but his vehicle rolled up and over me like a jet on Top Gun. Jesus wore racing goggles, and his hair blew backward in the wind as he laughed!

Wax Your Surfboard

This week in Heaven, Jesus and I were standing on a beach as he showed me a tidal wave. It was taller than a building and it was rolling in toward us.

He said, "You could swim in front of it," (which didn't seem like a good idea). Or, he said that I could surf with him on top of it. Instantly, we both had large waxed surfboards, and were surfing on top of this vast wave coming to shore.

Jesus said, "You always have choices when the waves come. Either stand on the beach in fear and watch it hit, or try to out-swim it with a lot of effort, or just wax your surfboard and ride on top with ME and with no worries."

His message to me was, "Trust God. Do what he tells you to do, trust him, praise him, and go on vacation with your grandkids without fear."

Skateboards

I saw Jesus crouched down, skateboarding past people on the sidewalks of New York. Next, I saw him skateboarding on the sidewalks of California near the beach. I asked him why he was skateboarding.

Jesus said, "Because I like it."

He laughed saying, "Skateboarding, surfing, or even swinging in a park is very freeing; all worries leave."

When trouble comes, go into his presence, get refreshed and then go out to the pasture for peace.

I am the Gateway (Door). To enter through me is to experience life, freedom, and satisfaction. (John 10:9 TPT)

Another Bible version says it something like this: "To enter through Jesus is to go in and go out, and find pasture."

Motorcycles in Heaven

After spending time worshipping Jesus, I stood beside him next to two motorcycles: a red one for me and a black one for Jesus. We got on and began to ride extremely fast down a road, but not actually on the road, we were hovering just above it as we traveled. We rode around corners, leaning over to the right and the left as we traveled.

Then, as Jesus was riding in front of me, he suddenly missed a corner and crashed into a tree!

My first thought was, "OH NO, I killed Jesus! I'm going to be in trouble."

Then I realized that that was, of course, impossible. I rode up to the tree that Jesus had hit and saw him sitting down beside it. He suddenly stood up and began belly laughing wholeheartedly. And then, instantly, his bike which was in pieces, came back together — perfectly!

Jesus got back on his bike, looked at me, and said, "That was fun! Are you ready to go again?"

Our motorcycles had no engines and used no gas. They seemed to use life from the air as fuel, or maybe they used light as fuel, I wasn't sure.

Chapter 10

Q & A Teaching on Encountering Heaven

What if all I see is blackness when I pray?

There are a number of issues that hinder us from having encounters with Jesus. We'll talk about some of them here:

A. What have others said?

Someone may have told us that we cannot see in the spirit, and maybe we believed it. But that's clearly a lie because as soon as we are in Christ, we are in God's Kingdom and have become one with him in the spiritual realm.

When we asked Jesus to be our Lord and Savior, his Holy Spirit entered and stayed with us. We became one with Him. Better to think, "What do the scriptures say?" than "What did a denomination or a religious upbringing teach me?"

> So when that day comes, you will know that I am living in the Father and that you are one with Me, for I will be living in you. (John 14:20 TPT)

> But the one who joins (welds, knits) himself to the Lord is mingled into one spirit with Him. (1 Corinthians 6:17 TPT with my words in brackets)

So, to overcome this thinking of not being able to "see" in the spirit, just repent for believing the lie, and break it off. Ask Jesus for a tool to break down or break through that black wall. And then trust what Jesus gives you to break it. Ask Jesus to help you use the tool. If it is a chainsaw, cut through it. If Jesus shows up on a tractor, you and Jesus can ride and bash through the wall together. Maybe he gives you a blow dryer or a shovel. Whatever tool he gives you, use it to eliminate the wall.

After the "seeing-black" wall is destroyed, take Jesus' hand by faith and ask him to show you what is on the other side. Trust what you see, trust your imagination. The Holy Spirit uses your sanctified imagination to speak to you and lead you.

B. God is Light, not Darkness

If all we see is "black", it could be that we have participated in a lot of darkness during our life, and maybe it was not our choice.

Thank God we DO have a choice to release the darkness that we have participated in, by asking the Holy Spirit to forgive us for things we have seen and heard, and to forgive us for allowing into our eyes and ears things which polluted our imagination. Our eyes and ears are what Heaven calls portals, doors, or entryways; if those are not protected then harassing demonic thoughts and images can enter into our lives.

It's time to release the anger and hatred we may have been holding onto. It's time to release the jealousy we may have harbored. Let all the bitterness and fears go. Let his light shine in the dark corners, and get totally free and made whole.

Jesus is coming back for a spotless bride, not a Dalmatian.

I pray that the light of God will illuminate the eyes of your imagination, flooding you with light until you experience the full revelation of the hope of his calling. That is the wealth of God's glorious inheritances that he finds in us, his holy ones. (Eph. 1:18 TPT)

Repeat this prayer with me:

"Holy Spirit, I repent for the things I have seen and listened to, either willingly or unwillingly. I ask that you purify my eyes; the eyes of my imagination, and the eyes of my heart. I ask that you purify my ears and mouth. I receive the fire of the Holy Spirit to burn out all ungodly images, words, and thoughts. Holy Spirit, fill me now with your presence and your holiness. Thank you for purifying my imagination. Now, use the eyes of my heart and the eyes of my imagination for You and only You. I want to be filled with thoughts of eternal things like it says in Colossians 3:2."

Yes, feast on all the treasures of the Heavenly realm and fill your thoughts with Heavenly realities, and not with the distractions of the natural realm. (Col. 3:2 TPT)

C. Make the Trade

If all we see is "black", maybe the eyes of our hearts (the eyes of our imagination) got closed because they are stuck in the past.

We may have made a vow to ourselves in the past to never see or feel again because of witchcraft that we observed. Or maybe we were forced to participate in witchcraft. Having harsh words spoken to us, or seeing dark pictures with torment from the past may have caused us to feel abandoned. All those can make us not want to look for Jesus in an encounter.

It's time to make the trade.

Their minds are dull and slow to perceive, their ears are plugged and are hard of hearing, and they have deliberately shut their eyes to the truth. Otherwise, they would open their eyes to see, ears to hear, and minds to understand. Then they would turn to Me, and I would instantly heal them. (Matthew 13:15 TPT)

If your mind feels waterlogged and your ears are soaked with words from the past, let's get healed and set free.

Repeat this prayer with me:

"Holy Spirit, I ask for your fire to purify my memory, imagination, and thoughts. I trade the thoughts of death and suicide, fear of living, and fear of life, and I receive life and thoughts of life from you. I trade 'lack and hopelessness' for 'a good future and hope.' I trade and give you the past spirit of control and manipulation for freedom. Thank you, Holy Spirit, for setting me free. I ask that you show me what Jesus and Heaven look like right now."

> Yes, feast on all the treasures of the Heavenly realm and fill your thoughts with Heavenly realities, not with the distractions of the natural realm. (Colossians 3:2-3 TPT)

> So we look not at the things which are seen, but at the things which are unseen; for the things which are visible are temporal [just brief and fleeting], but the things which are invisible are everlasting and imperishable. (2 Corinthians 4:18 AMP)

D. But what if I hate men?

If all we see is "black," maybe we have hatred towards another person.

I had been counseling a Christian lady once who was overwhelmed with feelings of hatred for her husband, and she'd experienced many health struggles. I prayed with her and not long after that the Holy Spirit woke me at around 3 o'clock in the morning with this revelation:

"Hate in your soul for men will lodge in your body's cells."

Hate in our souls affects the eyes of our imagination (the eyes of our heart), and it will harden our hearts to the things of God. God doesn't hate! There is no hatred in God. He actively opposes "hate." The Bible wants us to trust God, Jesus, and the Holy Spirit.

Perhaps we've watched TV sitcoms or movies that portrayed men as untrustworthy, alcoholics, and gamblers; and that is what taught us to hate men. Maybe our moms had a bad relationship with men.

If you have unwanted voices in your mind, it could be that a generational hatred was passed down to you. Are you hearing your mother's voice from the past, for example, saying, "I hate the fact he can't fix anything, he doesn't know what screwdriver to use. I hate that he can't find the milk behind the mustard. I hate when he says my cooking is 'edible'. I hate how he always has control of the remote control, and I hate how he tells me how to park... ." If so, then don't wonder why you hate your spouse.

The Holy Spirit is trying to show us visions of Jesus as our loving husband. He is telling us that Jesus wants to have a relationship and spend time with us. But because the hatred and bitterness are taking space in our souls, we can't receive. Sometimes we are unaware of why we feel the way we do until the Holy Spirit shines the light on our "spot".

It's time to get the darkness out and release all hatred. It's time to allow the light of God to illuminate the darkness, time to cleanse our souls of all the dark spots. God is light, and he has no darkness in him. Light can't exist without the power that creates it — and the Holy Spirit is that power.

The hate and generational tendencies we got from parents and social media must be renounced and broken. We must break the vow that was made, and trade hate for love. So give God the hate in your soul and be healed and set free. Cast down every vain imagination from your heart and mind, and ask God to fill the eyes of your heart with images of Heaven's love and joy. Our eyes need to be purified so we can see our spouse through God's eyes.

> But if we freely admit our sins when His light uncovers them, He will be faithful to forgive us every time. God is just to forgive us our sins because of Christ, and He will continue to cleanse us from all unrighteousness. (1 John 1:9 TPT)

Repeat this prayer with me:

"I command all hatred for my spouse to leave me now. I command it to leave my bones, and every cell, every tissue in my body now. I repent for every word I have spoken against them. I receive love for them now. I receive the light of the Holy Spirit into my imagination to purify my thoughts and heart, and cleanse me. Lord, fill my thoughts with Heavenly activity that is full of joy, celebration, love, and life."

E. Is it okay to have Heavenly encounters? (um YES!)

> And now we are brothers and sisters in God's family because of the blood of Jesus, and He (Jesus) welcomes us to come into the most holy sanctuary in the Heavenly realm — boldly and without hesitation. v.20 For He (Jesus) has dedicated a new, life-giving way for us to approach God. For just as the veil was torn in two, Jesus' body was torn open to give us free and fresh access to Him (God)! v.21 And since we now have a magnificent High Priest (Jesus) to welcome us into God's house, v.22 we come closer to God and approach Him with an open heart, fully convinced that nothing will keep us at a distance from Him (God). For our hearts have been sprinkled with blood to remove impurity, and we have

been freed from an accusing conscience. Now, we are clean, unstained, and presentable to God inside and out! (Hebrews 10:19-22 TPT)

The veil in the temple was torn from top to bottom, symbolizing that as Jesus' back was being ripped open, Jesus made the way for us to step over into the Holy of Holiness. Jesus paid the price, just as a spotless, unblemished lamb would. His back didn't look like a small bedsore to give us a symbolic peephole, to peek into the Holy of Holies. No, his back was torn wide open so we could boldly come into God's house.

Because of the Blood of Jesus, God our Father welcomes us to come closer to Him, and approach Him. We are fully convinced that nothing will keep us apart — except our minds. If someone told you not to look at God, or approach him, or to never have experiences with him in Heaven, remember what you just read above in Hebrews 10:19-22, and forgive those who told you these things. Release the bitterness and lies you have been taught and accept that Jesus paid for it all. Trust the Holy Spirit's leading to step into God's presence.

F. How Do We Access Heaven?

The first way is by faith. By just believing we are already there. We are seated with Jesus in Heaven. Some call it "co-seated" which means we have the authority to be there.

> He raised us up with Christ the exalted One, and we ascended with him into the glorious perfection and authority of the Heavenly realm, for we are now co-seated as one with Christ! (Ephesians 2:6 TPT)

The second way is through God's sovereign act. A "sovereign act of God" means he pulls on you, and you can feel a drawing from God. It's like you can't wait to leave work and get home, so you can come away and be with him. He pulls on your spirit-man like a lover draws on your heart to go away to be alone, just the two of you.

As you follow and obey that pulling or drawing, the encounters will get more vivid, in color, and authenticity. Not that other encounters are not authentic, but this kind of drawing is a step closer to him, and it's hard to explain the love you experience.

John describes this drawing (to come up here) in the following verse:

> After these things I looked, and behold, a door standing open in Heaven, and the first voice which I had heard, like the sound of a trumpet speaking with me, said, "Come up here, and I will show you what must take place after these things." Immediately I was in the Spirit; and behold, a throne was standing in Heaven, and someone was sitting on the throne. (Revelation 4:1-2 NASB)

Note that the door to Heaven is standing open. And that means it is in its permanent position; you can stop knocking and just go through the door. Then when you go through, you "look" — but you must look to SEE. It's like opening the refrigerator door to look for the milk. You might be looking, but you are still not seeing the milk. When you get to the door, look around to see what you can see — and trust what you "think" you are seeing.

Then when you return from the encounter, please write it down and ask the Holy Spirit questions. You may ask him, "What do you want me to take away from this encounter?" "What do you want me to bring back to Earth from this?"

Also ask yourself these questions: "What did I see, feel, smell, hear? What shoes was Jesus wearing? What clothes did he have on? How was his hair fixed?" By faith, you believe in what you see.

G. Can someone really SEE God?

No one has ever gazed upon the fullness of God's splendor except the uniquely beloved Son, who is cherished by the Father (from the lap of the Father) and held close to His heart. Now he (Jesus) has unfolded to us (lead the way) the full explanation of who God truly is. (from 1 John 4:12 and John 1:18 TPT)

Jesus gazed upon the fullness of God from the Father's lap. He was and is being held in close intimacy with the Father. By his death, shed blood and resurrection, Jesus led the way to the Father's lap, right next to his heart. So, where are we seated? We are seated in Jesus, right next to the Father. If you are seated that close, then wouldn't you be able to see God?

So when that day comes, you will know that I am living in the Father and that you are one with me, for I will be living in you. (John 14:20 TPT)

Jesus is in the Father and you are in Jesus. You are seated on the Father's lap, being held close to his heart. You are also seated with Jesus on the throne.

H. Should I even want to see into the Heavenly realm?

Christ's resurrection is your resurrection, too. This is why we are to yearn/desire for all that is above, for that's where Christ sits, enthroned at the place of all power, honor, and authority. Yes, feast on all the treasures of the Heavenly realm and fill your thoughts with Heavenly realities and not with the distractions of the natural realm. Your crucifixion with Christ has severed the TIE to this life, and now your true life is hidden away in God in Christ. (Colossians 3:1-3 TPT)

That scripture says we are to yearn or desire for all that is above. To feast on all the treasures of the Heavenly realm. Your tie to this life has been severed. This doesn't mean you should sit on the couch and do nothing. This doesn't mean you should not participate in your children's schools or the government. You are to do what God has called you to do. If he has called you to sing, then sing. You can also homeschool your children, paint, garden, or do whatever he has called you to do.

All this means that we are not tied to this realm alone; we CAN go ahead and feast on the things in the Heavenly realm. Our true life is hidden away in Christ.

I. How do I see more?

You can see more by practicing his presence more. Each time you encounter Jesus, know that he has so much more to show you.

> But solid food is for the [spiritually] mature, whose senses are trained by practice to distinguish between what is morally good and what is evil. (Hebrews 5:14 AMP)

Spend time in God's presence and under the Holy Spirit's leading. Practice what your eyes and ears perceive and how the atmosphere feels. Your spiritual senses of seeing, hearing, touching or feeling, tasting, and smelling, are trained by practice. And, please write it down. Then ask Holy Spirit if it lines up with scripture or God's character?

J. Do I have to dance, sing, quote scriptures, or fast to see Jesus?

You can encounter Jesus as regularly and as often as you take the time to come away and get quiet.

Jesus said to me, "Not everyone wants to stop and be with me. They want to 'do for me,' not 'be with me.' ... Be with me now, there's always time to 'do' — but for now, 'be.'"

I encourage you to set aside time to be with Jesus. Put on some soaking music and focus on Jesus. Focus on Jesus' face and worship him so you can quiet your body and mind. You may begin by reading scripture and praying in tongues. Keep a paper and pen close by so that when natural things come to mind (like things you need to do), you can jot them down to get them out of your head — and then go right back to worshipping Jesus.

You must slow down. This intimate time with Jesus isn't to be rushed. Wait until you feel a change in the atmosphere, until you feel the heavy presence of God, or a sweet tenderness enter the room. Trust the Holy Spirit's leading. Trust what you hear and what you see in your sanctified imagination.

Jesus may take you to the Father. The Father can come to you in a form where you can easily have a relationship with him — yes, the God of the Universe will come to you!

Jesus died and was beaten beyond recognition for YOU! The veil was torn so YOU could have access to the Father. The Father has made a way for you to come to him through Jesus. HE WANTS YOU TO COME TO HIM!

> Therefore, believers, since we have confidence and full freedom to enter the Holy Place [the place where God dwells] by [means of] the blood of Jesus, 20 by this new and living way which He initiated and opened for us through the veil [as in the Holy of Holies], that is, through His flesh, 21 and since we have a great and wonderful Priest [Who rules] over the house of God, 22 let us approach [God] with a true and sincere heart in unqualified assurance of faith, having had our hearts sprinkled clean from an evil conscience and our bodies washed with pure water. (Hebrews 10:19-22 AMP)

The blood of Jesus has made us righteous enough. It's not by our works but by Jesus' blood that we have these encounters. But we do have to come away, get quiet, and trust.

K. A Quiet Place with God

I encourage you to retreat to a quiet place. This is why I go camping and move my office out of my prayer room into its own space. The Holy Spirit wants to reveal God's secrets, but you must first quiet your mind.

> But just as it is written [in Scripture], "Things which the eye has not seen and the ear has not heard, And which have not entered the heart of man, All that God has prepared for those who love Him [who hold Him in affectionate reverence, who obey Him, and who gratefully recognize the benefits that He has bestowed]." 10 For God has unveiled them and revealed them to us through the [Holy] Spirit; for the Spirit searches all things [diligently], even [sounding and measuring] the [profound] depths of God [the divine counsels and things far beyond human understanding]. (1 Cor. 2:9-10 AMP)

One time when I went camping, my husband asked me, "What will you do?" I told him I wasn't going to do anything. I was going to do nothing! Some people feel like they are not loved or valued by God if they are not doing something; if they're not writing, answering emails, or counseling someone. But God wants us to be free from needing to do things, and to learn to enjoy being with him in the quiet times. He wants his children to come away and just be.

I want to be with him, talk to him, and listen to him (not to Rumble, YouTube, Facebook, or a podcast). Turn off the noise and listen to the Holy Spirit. He wants to reveal the thoughts and secrets of God's heart. Spending time with him increases your love for him.

Call to Me, and I will answer you, and tell you [and even show you] great and mighty things, [things which have been confined and hidden], which you do not know and understand and cannot distinguish. (Jeremiah 33:3 AMP)

Loving me empowers you to obey my commands. (John 14:15 TPT)

I pray these discussions will help to answer some of your questions. You may check out my YouTube channel or my website for more teachings. www.Heavenisfun.com

Remember, Jesus is coming soon!

More info about Kim

The Holy Spirit has been taking Kim to Heaven since 1988. Jesus shows her amazing people, places and things, and she sees lots of children there.

Kim leads Sozo Ministry; healing hearts is her passion. She has written several books about her experiences in Heaven:

1. *Heaven is still Fun* (More experiences Kim has had in Heaven)

2. *Heaven is Real and Fun* (Experiences Kim had in Heaven)

2. *How to Access Jesus in the Heavenly Realm Manual* (How you too can experience these things)

3. *Jesus is Real and Fun* (A children's activity coloring book about Heaven)

4. *Jesus Sat on a Stump* (A book dedicated to all the children that have been aborted or miscarried)

5. *Fuzzy Bunny and Smiling Monkey* (A children's bedtime story told to Kim by Jesus)

Please "Like" us on Facebook: Heaven is Real and Fun
You can order Kim's books at her website:
www.heavenisfun.com

Made in United States
Troutdale, OR
06/15/2025

32078054R00070